THE SPIRIT SPEAKS IN US

The Spirit Speaks In Us

Personal Prayer in The New Testament

by John Sheets, S.J.

DIMENSION BOOKS
DENVILLE, NEW JERSEY

This Edition Published January 1969.

Published by Dimension Books
Denville, New Jersey

Library of Congress Catalog Card Number: 68-31391
Copyright © 1968 by John Sheets

Nihil Obstat

Imprimatur

Monsignor James T. Clarke
Censor Librorum
July 30, 1968

Bishop J. Carroll McCormick
Bishop of Scranton
July 30, 1968

Table of Contents

Preface   9

Introduction   13

PART I. THE PRAYER OF CHRIST
1. The Prayer of Christ in the Synoptics   25
2. The Content of the Prayer of Christ in the Synoptics   47
3. The Prayer of Christ in the Gospel of St. John   59
4. The Prayer of Christ in the Letter to the Hebrews   67

PART II. THE PRAYER OF THE CHRISTIAN
1. The Prayer of the Christian in the Synoptics   77
2. The Prayer of the Christian in the Gospel of St. John   99
3. The Prayer of the Christian in the Acts
   of the Apostles   105
4. The Prayer of the Christian in the Apocalypse   113
5. The Prayer of the Christian in the Letters of St.Paul   125
6. The Prayer of the Christian as found in the Letters
   to all Christians   195
7. Conclusion   201

Introduction

THE SPIRIT SPEAKS IN US

The Christian community, as we find it described in the New Testament, was a community of prayer. This is a fact which is simply taken for granted. Though we find there many exhortations to pray, these are not usually exhortations to pray as contrasted with not praying, but rather exhortations to pray more. For a Christian to be was to pray, but to pray always "in the Lord."

Further, prayer was taken for granted among the pagans to whom the Gospel was preached. When they accepted the Gospel and were baptized, their prayer also was baptized, and took the orientation that belongs uniquely to Christian prayer. Much closer to the prayer of the Christian was the prayer of the Jews. Christian prayer drew heavily on the riches of the spiritual tradition of Israel.

We preface this study of the New Testament notion of prayer with these few remarks to recall the atmosphere in which Christianity was preached. It was a religious, prayerful atmosphere, though this atmosphere was contaminated with the errors of paganism. Christian prayer did not have to create a totally new atmosphere. Rather, like streaks of light piercing a cloudy sky, it had to purify and illumine this atmosphere.

Another atmosphere has moved over the world today. It is an atmosphere which generally does not act as a supportive medium for prayer. This does not mean that Christians are more prayerful or less prayerful than they used to be. Such comparisons are impossible and of doubtful validity. However, as T.S. Eliot remarks in one of his poems, in other ages men left God for other gods, but today they have left God for no god at all. This means that an a-religious atmosphere has settled over a great part of the western world. It is not an atmosphere which fosters prayer.

The interest shown today in some circles in the prayer of the Orient bears witness first of all to the need the human heart has for prayer, and secondly to the strange phenomenon that an exotic plant from the East has to be transplanted into Western soil in order to satisfy that need.

The pages which follow are a simple declaration, through the New Testament itself, that to be Christian is to be prayerful. There is no attempt to develop an elaborate theology of prayer, or to discuss the stages or history or types of prayer. Christian tradition has given us many books which are concerned with these subjects. The New Testament presents us with the Christian community at the very dawn of its existence, living in the presence of the risen Christ, praying its Maranatha, that the Lord come. In other words, the New Testament presents us with the Christian community as a community of prayer. The winds of culture can be warm or cold, friendly or hostile to prayer, but the Christian community still lives in the presence of the risen Christ, and prays for his coming. It will always be the community of prayer until its prayer is answered—when the Lord comes.

My thanks are due especially to those who organized the Scriptural Institute at Barat College in Lake Forest, Illinois, where the substance of this book was given as lectures. This Institute was organized and sponsored by the Adult Education Program of the Archdiocese of Chicago. Thanks are also due to the Benedictine Sisters of Mount Marty College in Yankton, South Dakota, who ministered to my needs in the heat of the day,

PREFACE

while I was preparing these lectures. I owe a particular debt of gratitude to Sister Jeremy Hall, O.S.B., of the College of St. Benedict, for her help in the preparation of the manuscript, and to Betty Jo Maly who suggested the title for the book.

Introduction

Before we begin our study of prayer in the New Testament it will be helpful if we set down the premises which form the framework within which our investigation will be carried on. If these premises are kept in mind, both the nature of our investigation as well as its limits will be better understood.

We assume, first of all, that prayer brings to a personal focus a life which is larger than prayer itself, namely, the religious life of a person as well as the religious life of a people. This is something which is obvious, but sometimes it is helpful to recall even the obvious. The prayer life has the same contours which belong to overall structures of the religious life of a person or a people. It simply brings these structures to a personal, conscious focus. This same idea is brought out through the ancient adage, *"Lex orandi, lex credendi.* The larger structure of our whole religious life is correlative to the structure which our prayer takes, and vice versa. "The law of our prayer is the law of our belief." This can be set down as the first premise which has to be presupposed in our study of the New Testament notion of prayer.

We assume, secondly, that there is a basic difference in the religious life (and therefore the prayer life) of a people for whom God is present as it were in a homogeneous or an undifferentiated fashion, and for the people for whom God is present in a way that shows election, choice, an entrance into their lives in an historical fashion. We are talking, of course, about the difference between the religion of Judaism and Christianity on the one hand, and those other religions of the world whose relationship with God (or the gods) is based upon God's undifferentiated presence in the world.

13

In Judaism and in Christianity prayer is not simply the manifestation of a natural awareness that man has of powers greater than himself, or of his dependence on these powers. Rather it is the response to God entering into their history. Prayer becomes a response to a word that was spoken, first of all through God's liberating action in their history, and secondly through the prophetic word which describes the significance of this action.

In Judaism and Christianity prayer is, then, obediential, partaking of and manifesting the very obedience that belongs to faith in God's word. It is in terms of obedience that belongs to the nature of faith that St. Paul describes his mission. "Through him (the Son) we received grace and our apostolic mission to preach the obedience of faith to all pagan nations in honor of his name" (Rm 1,5). Prayer is, then, truly a response, not to God's homogeneous presence in the processes of nature but to God's historical action in a people. Prayer is not the response (speaking of Jewish and Christian prayer) to the words resonating in man's mind or in nature. It is response to God's word spoken in time.

Jewish prayer and Christian prayer is always, therefore, by its nature related to time. It is not a-historical in the way in which natural mysticism by-passes or annuls time. By its very nature it is a response to the God who reveals himself through his action and through the word, particularly the prophetic word.

The revealing action of God and his revealing word are not simple declarations about truth or about truths. They are declarative in order to be imperative. God reveals himself in order to reveal his will for mankind. This takes place over the whole process of revelation.

His will is to give life to mankind. Ultimately the revelation culminates in the words, "God is love" (1 Jn 4,8).

Because God's word is imperative, the response of prayer is one that is obediential. It is attentive listening in the sense of a listening in order to do, not simply a listening in order to listen. It is not passive either in its stance of listening or in its preparedness to carry out what is hears. The whole of Christian prayer can be described as a listening, from the very beginning stages of prayer even to the heights of contemplation. The growth in prayer is marked by stages in the power to listen involving first of all the purification, which is necessary to listen, and then gradual development to the point where the one listening takes on more and more of the characteristics of the Word to whom he is listening, even to the point of a kind of identification which belongs to mystical prayer.

This then is the second assumption which runs through our treatment of prayer in the New Testament. Prayer in the Christian sense (building on but bringing to fruition the Jewish notion) is a response to God's word given to us in his freedom, where our response is both to the content of the word and to the will of God which lies behind the word. The gift of the word, our response, and the closer union brought about through opening oneself to the will of God are grace from beginning to end.

The third assumption is one that has to do with the relationship of the religion of Israel and the religion of Christianity, hence with the prayer of the Israelite and the prayer of the Christian. There is both a unity but also a radical discontinuity between the religious experience of Israel compared with that of the Christian. The unity comes from the fact that it is one and the same God who is the Emmanuel. It is one and the same God who freely turns towards man to draw him into a covenant relationship. The discontinuity comes from the fact of the Incarnation, which brings to fruition all that was contained in the Old Testament and yet its completeness also marks a full giving which is radical in its discontinuity with whatever gift preceded it. In one sense the Incarnation is along the same line as all of the other gifts of grace which preceded it and which depend on it. But in another sense it takes in everything along the line. It is not only the turning of God towards man through isolated acts throughout history, related though these acts are in the economy of salvation. It is the enfleshment of the very essence of God's-being-turned-towards-man. It is the very *totality* of the grace which constitutes the radical discontinuity.

The Christian life is a life in union with the Word-made-flesh. This takes place through the gift of the Spirit of Christ who creates a mysterious identity between the Christian and Christ, between the flesh of the risen Christ and the flesh of the Christian. The Christian is incorporated into the flesh of Christ chiefly through the sacraments of baptism and the eucharist. This is basically his covenant relationship. In Christ, through the gift of the Spirit, he is drawn into the relation of sonship.

In the Old Testament the ways of the people of God were to manifest the ways of God. As Moses said to God, "If indeed I have won your favor, please show me your ways, so that I can understand you and win your favor" (Ex 33,13). In the New Covenant the people of God do not live out the ways of God as he was known

16

in the Old Covenant. The Christian life is a living out of the ways of God-made-flesh in his passion, death, and resurrection.

The relationship of the religion of Christianity to that of Judaism serves to bring out the relationship of the prayer of the Christian to that of the Jew. There is both a unity but at the same time a radical discontinuity. The prayer of the Christian, like the whole life of the Christian, takes on the characteristics of sonship because of his union with the Word-made-flesh. This is what makes Christian prayer specifically distinct from any other kind of prayer. It is the prayer of one who is a son of the Father. Sonship here does not mean the same as in the Old Testament, where the nation or an individual could be called son of God. In the Christian there is, as it were, the consummation of the movement towards sonship which we see all through salvation history. But sonship can only be found in the consummated sense when the turning of God towards us is consummated in the Incarnation and Redemption. Only when the giving has been consummated is it possible for the sonship to be consummated.

But the consummation of this relationship is had through the relationship of the flesh of the Christian to the flesh of Christ. This is another way of saying that it is a sacramental relationship, where sonship is embodied in the flesh and given to us through fleshly means.

This then is the third assumption which underlies all that is said about the Christian notion of prayer. It is a listening with the heart of a son to the words of the Son who became flesh. It is a power to listen which comes from a sacramental union of the flesh of the Christian with the flesh of Christ. It is an openness to the will of

Christ behind the words of Christ, as this will is manifested to us in a sacramental way, in and through the Church.

Our final assumption or premise has to do with the Scripture itself and with the person of Christ who is described there. It is probably unnecessary to set this down since we presume that we are talking to a Christian audience. But it is helpful to recall once again that the writing of Scripture is charismatic writing. This is not the place to go into the nature of this charismatic writing which we call inspired writing. It is our purpose simply to recall that it is part of the whole economy of salvation. What characterizes this economy of salvation is the movement of God towards us. He does this through the complexus of events which make up the formation of the people of God of the Old Testament, through the prophets, through inspired words, and finally this movement of God towards us is, as it were, exhausted in the movement which we call the Incarnation and Redemption. The Scripture is one aspect of this movement of God towards us and is of a piece with the whole of his turning towards us.

The inspired words of the New Testament attempt to recapture the experience which the Apostles and the early Christian community had of Christ and his message. We should be as grateful to the New Testament writers for what they do *not* say as we are for what they *do* say about Christ. What they say is always conditioned by the awareness they have of the mystery of Christ, that his meaning far surpasses any words. There is the awareness that if everything were written, "The world itself, I suppose, would not hold all the books that would have to be written" (Jn 21,25.). They do not succumb to the temptation to put Jesus in a category familiar to them. Others might say that he was John the Baptist, or Elijah, or Jeremiah, or one of the prophets. But the writers of the New Testament confess, like Peter himself, that he is the Christ, the Son of the living God (Mt 16,14). They are aware that they cannot reduce Jesus to a category which is known from their contact with other men, no matter how religious they might have been. They prefer to let the mystery of Christ's presence speak not only through what they say but through what they leave unsaid.

This seems to be true in a particular way in what the gospels say about the prayer of Christ. The gospels speak often of the prayer of Christ, as we shall see. But they say more in what they leave unsaid. We have the feeling that what the gospels say about the prayer of Christ resembles the little eddies and currents which move around the familiar shore. We have some sense of the depth and intensity of the current far out in the middle of the river but to describe it lies beyond our power.

Those are the assumptions, then, which guide our study of the New Testament notion of prayer. With these in mind it might be easier for the New Testament to speak directly to us enabling us to see that prayer is as natural to the Christian life as breathing is to the living body.

We would like to conclude these introductory remarks by making some observations about the *personal* nature of prayer as in the New Testament.

All prayer is specified by the way in which a person or a people conceives its relationship to God or to the gods. Where this relationship is impersonal, prayer is reduced to magical formulas or rites. The instinct which gives rise to prayer is genuine, but prayer takes the contours of the life of worship of a people. If this worship is impersonal, the prayer itself is impersonal. Where God or the gods are seen as set over against mankind, prayer becomes a way of winning the favor of these divine powers much in the same way that men win the favor of a human sovereign who is looked upon as set over against the people. It is largely a *quid pro quo* relationship, one in which something is given with the expectation of something in return. It has little to do with the disposition of the heart, unless the disposition of the heart would affect the *quid pro quo* relationship.

Where the relationship to God is seen in terms that are personal, prayer becomes the register of the degree to which this personal relationship is realized. God is not seen as set over against mankind but rather as entering into communion with men. This, of course, is the meaning of the covenantal relationship in the Old Testament, and of its fulfilment in the New.

Our prayer, therefore, is specified by our notion of God, whether God is seen as a God who wills co-existence, or a God who wills communion. Further, our prayer is specified by our awareness of our needs, and an awareness that God can fulfill these needs in some way.

There is an awareness not only of our physical needs, the need for "our daily bread." There is the awareness of the need which we have to acknowledge God's otherness through our adoration, the need which we have to acknowledge our sins through sorrow, and an awareness that we have to acknowledge God's benefits in the past through thanksgiving. These characteristics of prayer can be found among any religious people, whether Christian or not.

It is precisely here, however, that we realize the uniqueness of the prayer of Israel (and even more so of Christian prayer), though this prayer has instincts and forms which are common to other peoples. The prayer of the Israelite arises because God has approached the people of Israel, not because they had approached God. It is this awareness which takes their worship and their prayer out of the realm of co-existence into that of communion. It is the awareness of God's kindness, his love, in approaching them, that converts their worship and their prayer from an impersonal response to one that is highly personal. God has personally entered into their lives and bound them to himself in a covenant relationship.

We find this personal quality throughout the prayer and worship of the Old Testament. We see it, for example, in the relationship of God and Moses. "God spoke to Moses as to a friend, face to face" (Ex 33,11). When God revealed his name to Moses, he opened the inner sanctuary of prayer. No greater invitation to prayer could be given than by revealing his name, a revelation of his inmost being.

The implications of God's turning towards them in a covenant relationship were not realized all at once. As these implications were realized in the course of their history, the life of worship and of prayer would register these changes. There is a gradual unfolding of God's will for them. This means that there is the gradual realization of the correlative of God's will, that is, of their own need. Basically the revelation of God's will for man is at the same time the revelation of man's greatest need. In the early stages of their history the Israelites realize their need for all that can sustain their life as a people. These needs are seen largely on a physical plane, for whatever would sustain their lives and be a protection against their enemies. Later in their history, while their physical needs are not forgotten, there is an awareness of a need for life which goes beyond the satisfaction of these physical needs. The sustained communion in the covenant led them to the realization of the need for God's own life, which is his holiness.

Holiness is not simply an attribute of God. It is the very center of God's life. At the root of God's will to enter into a covenant with the people was his will to communicate his holiness in and through the covenant relationship. The need and the desire for this holiness, for this life of God, reaches high points of intensity, as we find in many of the psalms (cf. Ps 42; 63; 84). We could say that the whole of revelation is directed to the unveiling of God's will to give his life to man, and at the same time the exposing of man's need for this life.

The final revelation of God's will to give his life and also the ultimate exposure of man's need is that which takes place through the Incarnation and Redemption. If the ultimate stage of revelation is the unveiling of God as a mystery of love, it is at the same time the exposing of the fact that man cannot exist without this love. Putting it more positively, it is the exposing of the fact that man's need is to live as a son of God—forever. It is only when Christ is revealed as the source of the living water that one also understands that man's thirst is for this living water which overflows into life everlasting. Man has many thirsts, many needs, but at the root of all of them, and enveloping them all, is the thirst for life forever, with the Son.

Christian prayer comes forth from a thirst for this life with the Son. We can dare to pray in this way only because we are indeed sons. We can enter God's presence with the confidence which comes from the fact that we are brothers of Christ. Christian prayer is specified, then, by its relationship to the Son. In him the will of the Father to give us his life was revealed; in him the need which we have for this life was exposed; in him there is now the fulness of this life. Through the gift of his Spirit we are made aware of our need and are empowered to pray for the fulfilment of the need.

There is, then, a constant development which marks the prayer of a covenanted people. This development moves in rhythm with the development of the meaning of salvation, going, as was said, from a notion of salvation which had to do with this life to the notion of salvation as life forever with the Son. Old Testament prayer was open-ended, waiting for the fulness of the revelation of God's will to give life and the depths of our need to receive this life. The full meaning of prayer is made possible only when the full meaning of salvation is revealed, that is, when we learn that eternal life means to know the only God and Jesus Christ whom he has sent (Jn 17, 3).

Lest personal prayer, and the development of personal prayer among the covenanted people be regarded in too individualistic a fashion, it is helpful to recall that prayer looked not only to the fulfilment of one's own needs but to the fulfilment of the needs of the other members of the covenant. There is, in other words, a growing awareness of the intercessory power of prayer. This is found early in Hebrew history. We find examples of intercessory prayer in Abraham, Jacob, and Moses (cf. Gn 18,22-33; 28,20-22; Ex 5, 22-23; 32, 11-14; Nb 11, 1-5). We find the most developed expression of intercessory prayer in the prayer of the Suffering Servant who prayed for sinners (Is 53, 12).

But again it is in the New Testament that we find the revelation of the power of the prayer of intercession. In Christ there is the fulness of the power to intercede. This comes from his union with the will of the Father, and at the same time his complete identification with the needs of those for whom he is praying. "In the days of his earthly life he offered up prayers and petitions, with loud cries and tears, to God who was able to deliver him from the grave. Because of his humble submission his prayer was heard" (Heb 5,7).

The Christian shares in this new power to intercede. His prayer includes not only those who belong to the people of the covenant but it takes in all peoples. "My advice is that, first of all, there should be prayers offered for everyone" (1 Tm 2, 1).

With these ideas serving as an introduction we hope that the New Testament can speak about Christian prayer through the simplicity of its own testimony, without a great deal of commentary.

We shall treat the subject by dividing it into two main divisions, taking first of all the prayer of Christ, and then the prayer of the Christian.

PART I. THE PRAYER OF CHRIST

1. THE PRAYER OF CHRIST IN THE SYNOPTICS

In our study of the prayer of Christ in the synoptics we shall limit ourselves mainly to the Gospel of St. Luke, but we will note the passages where the other synoptics differ from Luke's account.

Luke has a special interest in the prayer of Christ. This is evident in several places where he deliberately completes Mark's description of an event by adding the observation that Jesus was praying. Mark records the fact that Jesus prayed at key moments in his public life. Luke's gospel, on the other hand, creates the impression that the whole of Jesus' life was conducted in an atmosphere of prayer. His prayer was not limited to certain key moments which had to do with the establishing of his kingdom. Rather these key moments were seen as privileged moments of what was a constant atmosphere.

It would perhaps serve the interests of economy of space and time simply to note the references to the texts without quoting them. But something of the impact of our study would be lost unless we quote the text as fully as possible. In this way the New Testament witness to the meaning of the prayer of Christ and the prayer of the Christian can have its greatest efficacy.

The first reference which we find to the prayer of Christ is one that is indirect. It is the account of the finding of Jesus in the temple (Lk 2, 41-52). The temple was a privileged place of prayer. Christ described it as such when he drove those who were trading out of the temple, "Then he went into the temple and began driving out the traders, with these words, 'Scripture says, "My house shall be a house of prayer; but you have made it a robbers' cave" ' " (Lk 19, 45-46).

Before Luke described the finding of Jesus in the temple, he had already spoken of it as a place of prayer. When he describes Zechariah at his priestly ministry in the sanctuary, he mentions that "The whole congregation was at prayer outside" (Lk 1, 10). Simeon met the anointed of God in the temple and began to praise God. "Guided by the Spirit he came into the temple; and when the parents brought in the child Jesus to do for him what was customary under the Law, he took him in his arms, and praised God." There follows the prayer of praise of Simeon. "Now, Master, you can let your servant go in peace, just as you promised; because my eyes have seen the salvation which you have prepared for all the nations to see, a light to enlighten the pagans and the glory of your people Israel" (Lk 2, 27-32). His words are both a prayer and a prophecy. It is possible to hear the voice of the Israel of God in the words of Simeon at the very moment when the fulfilment which had been promised in the past was revealed as a present actuality. Spoken from within the temple, where God met the faithful Israelite in worship, the words speak of a fulfilment which goes beyond the temple. This child will become the light which will enlighten the pagans. This child will be the glory of Israel. The glory of God will have a new abode, not in the temple but in the person of this child. In the Old Testament the glory of God was manifested chiefly through his presence in the temple; now it will be manifested in a person, this little child.

Then the words of Simeon take on an ominous tone. In a mysterious way the prophecy of fulfilment, of salvation, of light, and of glory is linked with another prophecy which has to do with frustration, darkness, and death. "You see this child: he is destined for the fall and for the rising of many in Israel, destined to be a sign that is rejected. And a sword will pierce your own soul too — so that the secret thoughts of many may be laid bare" (Lk 2, 34-35). These words referring to the rise and fall of many in Israel, have overtones which touch not only the existence of Israel but also of the temple, the symbol of God's presence among them.

Before the incident of the finding of the child Jesus in the temple, one other temple incident is described. Anna, the prophetess came by just at that moment and began to praise God; and she spoke of the child to all who looked forward to the deliverance of Jerusalem" (lk 2, 38). She lived in the presence of God in the temple. "She was now eighty-four years old and never left the temple, serving God night and day with fasting and prayer" (Lk 2, 37).

In this scene we catch a glimpse of the fulfilment of God's saving presence in the child who is presented in the temple. This child will be the saving presence of God to Israel, one which will not be entirely accepted. Some will rise, and some will fall because of him. But the incident is of interest to our present consideration of the prayer of Christ. Just as Anna never left the temple but served God night and day with fasting and prayer, so it is with Christ. Luke will show that the whole atmosphere of Christ's life is one that is lived within the temple precincts of God's presence. The temple, the symbol of God's presence to Israel, is now giving way to the reality foreshadowed by it. The reality is Christ.

We come then to the incident of the finding of Jesus in the temple. We cannot comment on all of the implications of this episode in our Lord's life. We are no doubt in the presence of one of those symbolic actions like those of the prophets. This passage is similar to the prologue of St. John's Gospel. Just as the prologue sets forth the themes of his gospel, here also the rest of Luke's Gospel has to be read in the light of this incident. Perhaps the full extent of the meaning escapes us, but at least the central idea is clear to us. The child Jesus claims a unique relationship to God, which means a unique relationship to the place where God is present, and a unique relationship to the work of God.

The incident takes place on the occasion of the celebration of the passover. This was the feast on which the Jews celebrated God's saving presence among them in delivering them from the bonds of slavery. We read that the parents of Jesus used to go up to Jerusalem every year for the feast of the passover. On this particular occasion when Jesus was twelve years old, they went up as usual for the feast, but Jesus remained behind. They returned to look for him. Luke gives us the impression that his parents looked everywhere else before they decided to look for him in the temple. "When they failed to find him they went back to Jerusalem looking for him everywhere" (Lk 2, 44). Finally they found him in the temple listening to the doctors and asking them questions. When his mother saw him, she said, "My child, why have you done this to us? See how worried your father and I have been, looking for you.' 'Why were you looking for me?' he replied, 'Did you not know that I must be busy with my Father's affairs?" Or as another translation has it, " 'Did you not know that I must be in my Father's house?' " (Lk 2, 48-50).

There are perhaps allusions to the Wisdom literature in this passage. In this literature Wisdom is described as being present to Israel in a particular way. This Wisdom is not something abstract. Rather it is God's life, his word, his spirit, his law which are present to Israel. It is possible that Luke wished to portray Christ as the incarnation of this wisdom (cf. Pr 8, 9).

But in any case it is clear that Jesus shows an awareness that the God who is present to the people of Israel in a special way in the temple is present to him in a most special way, as his own Father. He shows this awareness of God as his Father, of an intimate communion with God, in the place where God communicated with his people. When Jesus left the temple, and went down with his parents to Nazareth, he never really left the temple. He took the temple with him. He *is* the temple. He did not leave the place of communion with his Father. He himself is the place of communion. Later he will say, "Everything has been entrusted to me by my Father; and no one knows who the Son is except the Father; and who the Father is except the Son and those to whom the Son chooses to reveal him" (Lk 10, 22). This awareness is already in the child of twelve. The relationship with the Father and the Father's affairs creates the atmosphere which moves with him, whether he is in Jerusalem or in Nazareth or in the Garden of Gethsemani.

So far we have treated those passages which refer to the prayer of Christ only in an indirect way in so far as they point out his relationship to his Father. The first direct reference we have to the prayer of Jesus is in the description of his baptism. "During a general baptism of the people, when Jesus too had been baptized and was praying, heaven opened and the Holy Spirit descended on him in bodily form like a dove; and there came a voice from heaven, 'Thou art my Son, my Beloved; on thee my favor rests' " (Lk 3, 21-22).

Between the time when Jesus was found in the temple and the time of his baptism here described, no other event is interposed. In the former Jesus speaks of God as his Father, and here the Father speaks of Jesus as his beloved Son. The Holy Spirit in bodily form manifests this presence of the Father with the Son, a presence which is a loving communion. The text, "Thou art my Son, my Beloved; on thee my favor rests" recalls the Suffering Servant theme in the prophecies of Deutero-Isaiah. This communion of Father and Son is directed to the work which the Son has to accomplish. This is the work of the redemption.

We can picture Jesus praying by the side of the Jordan after his baptism. He is either kneeling, as was sometimes the posture, or standing with hands extended towards heaven, also a common posture for prayer. If we could probe the consciousness of Jesus at this moment, how could we describe his prayer? It is a prayer of deepest communion. But we have the feeling of standing on the side of a deep abyss. We hardly even have anything with which to measure the dimensions, far beyond anything we have experienced. The symbolic representation of the Holy Spirit suggests the degree of inner communion. Luke keeps a respectful silence. At other times he records the hymns of praise, as we find in the hymn of Mary, of Zechariah, and of Simeon. But here he says more by what he leaves unsaid than by anything he could possibly say. Later we shall try in some way to appreciate the content of the prayer of Jesus.

Immediately following the description of Jesus' baptism Luke gives the genealogy of Jesus. He begins with Joseph and ends with Adam, who is called son of God. The full implications of this go beyond the scope of our treatment, but there is a definite comparison and contrast between Jesus as son of the Father, the beloved Son, who will bring about the redemption of many, and the first Adam. God walked with the first Adam in paradise. But that union was broken through sin. The Son who is the beloved lives in uninterrupted communion with the Father. This union will never be diminished through sin or interrupted through death. In him the union of God with the whole of mankind will be restored. As God walked with Adam in Paradise, so the Father walks with the Son, though in union which is infinitely deeper. It is the walking with the Father that constitutes the constant prayerful atmosphere of Christ's life.

There follows the description of Jesus' fast and temptation in the desert. "Full of the Holy Spirit, Jesus returned from the Jordan, and for forty days was led by the Spirit up and down the wilderness and tempted by the devil" (Lk 4, 1-2). Though it was a time of isolation from the company of men, it was a time of intimate communion with God. The time was spent in prayer. We also see how in a human way his prayer was formed by the prescribed prayers for the Jews. The words which he used to answer the temptations of the devil were taken from the daily prayer prescribed for the Jews. They formed his spontaneous answer to the temptations.

This time of prayer in the wilderness was not a time of ecstatic communion with God after the fashion of the ecstasy of an oriental mystic. It was a time of prayer for his mission, and the temptations themselves were directed against his mission. Jesus' prayer was always apostolic. His union with the Father in his human consciousness had to share in his whole meaning: to be sent. Just as everything he did was an expression of his mission, so all of his prayer was an expression of this mission. Even in its intense union with the Father it remained "family prayer," prayer for those to whom he was sent.

"Then Jesus, armed with the power of the Spirit, returned to Galilee; and reports about him spread through the whole countryside. He taught in their synagogues and all men sang his praises. So he came to Nazareth, where he had been brought up, and went to the synagogue on the Sabbath day as he regularly did" (Lk 4, 14-16). Luke points out that it is the Spirit who is the source of Jesus' power. He also points out (an addition peculiar to Luke's account) that Jesus attended the synagogue regularly. This means that he took part in the regular prayer life of the community.

In the verses which follow there is a description of the opposition which he met from his fellow townsmen in Nazareth, then of the success of his preaching in Capernaum. After describing some of the cures which

Jesus worked, Luke says, "When day broke he went out and made his way to a lonely spot" (Lk 4, 42). Mark's account in this instance is more explicit in its reference to prayer. "Very early next morning he got up and went out. He went away to a lonely spot and remained there in prayer. But Simon and his companions searched him out, found him, and said, 'They are all looking for you.' He answered, 'Let us move on to the country towns in the neighborhood; I have to proclaim my message there also; that is what I came to do' " (Mk 1, 35-39). In this instance we find that Jesus retired to pray before he began his preaching to the other towns besides Nazareth and Capernaum.

Luke goes on to describe the great success of his mission. He mentions that Jesus would retire from time to time for prayer. "But the talk about him spread all the more; great crowds gathered to hear him and to be cured of their ailments. And from time to time he would withdraw to lonely places for prayer" (Lk 5, 15-16).

It would be a gross failure in our appreciation of the human consciousness of Jesus if we looked on his prayer simply as a way of giving example to the rest of us to pray. He retired to the lonely places to pray because he *needed* to pray. Yet we may ask: if he were in constant union with the Father and always doing the will of the Father, what need could there be for prayer which ostensibly took him apart from the work of establishing the kingdom? If we understand this as a real need, we might understand to some extent the meaning of the prayer of Jesus. It is not the need to be alone, which some of us feel when the business of the world gets too much for us. It is not the need that we feel because our work becomes distracting, and we have to retire in order to concentrate. Our need for prayer and solitude is prompted often by the fact that things just get to be too much for us. We have to clear them out of our vision if we are to see clearly for a few moments.

The need which Jesus felt for prayer was based on what he was. He was the Son, and the Father was his Father. His need for prayer did not come from some need to restore a power which was hemmed in, poured out, or dispersed through his activity for men. His need was the need that a Son has to be with his Father. There are basically two needs which make up the mystery of Jesus: his need to be with the Father, and his need to be with his brethren. These needs are not opposed. They are two aspects of one life, in perfect harmony with each other. Sometimes we see the need to be with the Father come to the fore; at other times his need to be with men. But again his need to be with the Father was not a need to withdraw from the company of men. He took men with him when he went into the period of quiet union with the Father. They were not left outside in some practical world which pertained to work and to action while he withdrew into some theoretical world of prayer. He brought them with him. This is particularly true of his prayer in the agony in the garden. He brought all men with him into that most lonely spot.

On one occasion the Pharisees and the lawyers challenged the conduct of Jesus' disciples, indirectly finding fault with Jesus' formation of the disciples. In his reply he mentions that his disciples do not have to fast or mourn now. The time will come for that. But he was careful not to say that they did not have to pray. "Then they said to him, 'John's disciples are much given to fasting and the practice of prayer, and so are the disciples of the Pharisees; but yours eat and drink' " (Lk 5, 33). Jesus said that the time for them to fast would come when the bridegroom would be taken from them. But he did not put any moratorium on their prayer.

After he cured the man with the withered arm on the Sabbath, we read that the Pharisees "were beside themselves with anger, and began to discuss among themselves what they could do to Jesus. During this time he went out one day into the hills to pray, and spent the night in prayer to God. When day broke he called his disciples to him, and from among them he choose twelve . . ." (Lk 6, 11-13). This is an instance where Luke completes Mark's account by adding the observation that Jesus prayed.

At the moment when it begins to be manifested that he would be taken away from them soon (Lk 5, 35; 6, 11), he takes the momentous step of choosing twelve disciples who will form the nucleus of his community. Like the twelve tribes of Israel they stand for the whole people of God of the New Covenant. Before he chose these men he spent the whole night in prayer. Undoubtedly his prayer was concerned with this major step in the formation of his kingdom. Perhaps it was during this night that he prayed his special prayer for Peter, "Simon, Simon! Satan, you must know, has got his wish to sift you all like wheat; but I have prayed for you, Simon, that your faith may not fail, and once you have recovered, you in your turn must strengthen your brothers" (Lk 22, 31).

The next references to the prayer of Jesus occur in chapter nine. After the apostles returned from their apostolic mission, Jesus took them aside with him. "and withdrew to a town called Bethsaida where they could be by themselves" (Lk 9, 10). But the crowds followed them. There follows the description of the multiplication of the five loaves and two fishes. This is done in a prayerful way. Jesus raised his eyes to heaven and said the blessing over the loaves and fishes. Then he broke them and handed them to his disciples to distribute among the crowd.

The next episode is one of those key moments in the foundation of his kingdom. As is customary it is preceded by prayer. "Now one day when he was praying alone in the presence of his disciples he put this question to them, 'Who do the crowds say I am?' " (Lk 9, 18). The disciples tell him the various opinions which people have. Then Peter makes his own confession, "You are the Christ of God" (Lk 9, 21).

TRANSFIGURATION

The description we find here differs from the others. Here Jesus is described as praying alone--but in the presence of his disciples. We never find any reference to his praying with his disciples. On the other hand if he took part in the synagogue services he must have prayed with the people and with his disciples who were also in attendance. When he is among his own, as master with his disciples, he never prays with them to the Father. He prays for them and he teaches them how to pray. But there is always the awareness that when he stands before the Father he is there as the only Son, and in this way there is an infinite distance between him and his disciples. At the same time he knows that he is standing *before* the Father only because he is there *for* men -- he is their mediator with the Father. Praying alone, but in the presence of his disciples -- this is the meaning of Christ as mediator. He joined in the public prayer of the people of Israel as one who belonged to the people of God. But in his private prayer he prayed not as one of a people, but as the only Son of the Father.

There follows the first prophecy of his passion. " 'The Son of Man' he said 'is destined to suffer grievously, to be rejected by the elders and chief priests and scribes and to be put to death, and to be raised up on the third day' " (Lk 9, 22). There can be no doubt that the thought of his passion was always the subject of his prayer, not simply in the sense that the thought of suffering is something which it is difficult to get off one's mind, but rather in the sense that it belonged to his mission as the Suffering Servant and that it would be the way in which his kingdom would be established.

"About eight days after this conversation he took Peter, John, and James with him and went up into the hills to pray. And while he was praying the appearance of his face changed and his clothes became dazzling white" (Lk 9, 28-29). The theophany takes place while Jesus is praying, just as the theophany surrounding his baptism took place while he was praying, when the voice of the Father was heard, and the presence of the Holy Spirit was seen in the form of a dove. Here at the Transfiguration the intimate union and communion was allowed to show itself in a visible way. There was the presence of the glory of God, showing itself not in the physical temple, but in and through the body of Jesus. The cloud symbolized the presence of the Holy Spirit. Then there was the voice of the Father, "This is my Son, my Chosen; listen to him" (Lk 9, 36).

We are again in the presence of a mystery which eludes analysis. For our purposes it is enough to bring out the fact that Jesus is rendered glorious while he is praying, and that the sign of the presence of the Holy Spirit and the approval of the Father are like an act of benediction over the praying figure of Jesus. Peter did not realize that Jesus' own level of existence, his own relationship to the Father, was infinitely different from that relationship which the prophets, Moses and Elijah, had. He wanted to make three tents, one for each of them. As Luke says, "He did not know what he was saying" (Lk 9, 33). The voice of the Father then tells them that this is his beloved Son. Though the full implications of that will not be realized until after Pentecost, the words put Jesus on an entirely different level from that of the greatest prophets of the Old Testament. There is a new tent in which the glory of God dwells. That is the very person of Jesus. When Jesus had told his parents, when they found him in the temple, that he had to be in his Father's house, they did not understand what he meant. We find out more clearly what those words mean in this mystery of the Transfiguration. He himself is the Father's house.

In chapter ten we have one of the few instances where we are allowed to catch a glimpse of the consciousness of Christ in his prayer. It takes place in an atmosphere of apostolic joy. The seventy-two had just returned from their apostolic mission and were filled with joy at their success. Jesus first cautioned them to discern the true cause of their joy from what was simply passing. Then, as if their own joy was contagious, Jesus himself began to rejoice. "At that moment Jesus exulted in the Holy Spirit and said, 'I thank thee, Father, Lord of heaven and earth, for hiding these things from the learned and wise, and, revealing them to the simple. Yes, Father, such was thy choice.' Then turning to his disciples he said. 'Everything is entrusted to me by my Father; and no one knows who the Son is but the Father, or who the Father is but the Son, and those to whom the Son may choose to reveal him.' Turning to his disciples in private he said, 'Happy the eyes that see what you are seeing! I tell you, many prophets and kings wished to see what you now see, yet never saw it; to hear what you hear, yet never heard it' " (Lk 10, 21-24).

We witness here a special manifestation of Christ's joy in the saving will of the Father. As always it takes place through the power of the Holy Spirit. The prayer is addressed to God, his Father. It is a prayer of thanks that the Father has revealed "these things" to the simple and has hid them from the learned of this world. What are "these things?" Jesus describes them when he turns to the disciples and tells them of the relationship of the Father to the Son and of the Son to the Father. He is the mediator of the will of the Father. He is the Lord of history, for all things have been entrusted to him. "These things" take in the whole economy of salvation as this economy is seen to come to its center in Christ. Ultimately "these things" are the revelation of the meaning of the Father himself. It will be summed up by St. John when he says "God is love."

This prayer of Christ stands apart from all the other examples we have of his prayer. It is to all effects a post-Resurrection or a post-Pentecost prayer. Jesus is filled with joy at the thought of what will be accomplished through his mission. For the moment the effort of his Passion is not in the forefront but rather the joy that comes from the realization of what will be accomplished through the saving will of the Father. He declares also that his disciples are happy—even though he said previously that they had to mourn. They are happy because they belong to his economy of salvation. They are happy because they have been chosen by the Father, just as Simon is declared happy or blessed, because the Father had chosen him (Mt 16, 17). This prayer is Jesus' "Magnificat." It is spoken from the vantage point of fulfilment rather than that of steps along the road to the fulfilment. He speaks from a heart which overflows with joy that comes from the presence by anticipation of the fruits of his redemptive act.

In chapter eleven there is again a description of Jesus at prayer. "Once, in a certain place, Jesus was at prayer. When he ceased, one of his disciples said, 'Lord, teach us to pray, as John taught his disciples.' He answered, 'When you pray, say . . .' " (Lk 11, 1-2) Jesus gave them the prayer which is called the "Lord's Prayer." We shall comment briefly on the contents of this prayer when we speak of the prayer of the Christian. We would simply like to note for the present that this prayer flows from the prayerfulness of Jesus. It shows how Jesus himself was so filled with the spirit of prayer that without any hesitation he could teach men a prayer which is noted for utter simplicity and its inexhaustible richness.

It is as if Jesus knew what each of us in our heart of hearts wanted to say; then he said it for us. This awareness of what we want to say comes from an awareness of what we need to say. He knew our needs, radically a need for God and his kingdom, but also the need for other men, and the need for our daily bread. The

40

"Lord's" prayer is really the prayer of each one of us. The notes were there but he composed the music.

An implicit reference to Jesus' prayer is found in chapter twenty-one. "His days were given to teaching in the temple; and then he would leave the city and spend the night on the hill called Olivet" (Lk 21, 37). These were the days when his mission was coming to a close. His passion and death were imminent. The words which he addressed to the crowds when he was speaking of the trials of the last days were certainly an indication of his own state of soul during these days. "Be on the alert, praying at all times for strength to pass safely through all these imminent troubles" (Lk 21, 36).

There is then in chapter twenty-two the description of his prayer at the last passover he ate with them. "Then he took bread, and blessed and broke it, and gave it to them, saying, 'This is my body, given for you; do this for a commemoration of me.' And so with the cup, when supper was ended, 'This cup,' he said, 'is the new testament in my blood which is to be shed for you'•" (Lk 22, 19-20). We can catch something of the spirit which lies behind these words of thanks or blessing when we appreciate the words he used to describe his attitude toward this supper. " 'How I have longed to eat this passover with you before my death' " (Lk 22, 15). We witnessed Christ's exultation when he anticipated the fulfilment which would come through his redemptive act (Lk 10, 21-22). There is something of the same note of fulfilment which is present here at the moment when he would institute the sacramental act which would carry out the revelation of his Father's love until the second coming. When he exulted in the Spirit over the fruition of God's plan, he was exulting over the marvelous design of the Father. Here he manifests his longing for that moment when he would give them the means to bring about that design of the Father.

When we come to the prayer of Jesus in the agony in the garden, we feel very much like the disciples. We are aware in some way that something important is taking place, but we feel like strangers and spectators watching a drama, which we know involves ourselves but which at the same time is beyond us. As far as possible we would like to have the words speak for themselves. "Then he went out and made his way as usual to the Mount of Olives, accompanied by the disciples. When he reached the place he said to them, 'Pray that you may be spared the hour of testing.' He himself withdrew from them about a stone's throw, knelt down, and began to pray, 'Father, if it be thy will, take this cup away from me. Yet not my will but thine be done.' And now there appeared to him an angel from heaven bringing him strength, and in anguish of spirit he prayed the more urgently; and his sweat was like clots of blood falling to the ground. When he rose from prayer and came to the disciples he found them asleep, worn out by grief. 'Why are you sleeping?' he said. 'Rise and pray that you may be spared the test' " (Lk 22, 39-46).

Here we have some indication of the communion which Jesus had both with the will of the Father and the needs of mankind. If it is the will of the Father that Jesus enter completely into the needs of mankind, even to the point of a complete assimilation of the consequences of man's sin, through his passion and death, then it is also the will of Jesus. Being in an intense agony he prayed even more urgently. Spiritual writers and mystics have tried to give us some notion of what took place in this dark hour of the prayer of Jesus. But we can only touch the surface.

Does not the heart of the conflict lie in the deep union which he has with the Father, a union which is always that of the beloved Son but at the same time a deliberate entering into that closedness which defines unredeemed human nature? The shock that comes from the collision of complete openness with the complete closedness taking place within one human consciousness, could only result in the deepest agony. There is the consciousness of his own sanctity through the fulness of the gift of the Spirit. On one occasion, when he realized one aspect of the redemption, that is man's openness to the will of God, he exulted in the Spirit. Now there is complete conscious awareness of man's closedness to this will of God. This awareness seeps into the whole of his consciousness. He begs that this chalice pass from him, unless it be the Father's will that he drink it. In one case it was a prayer of praise and of thanks. Here it is a prayer of petition. The conflict is more intense because of the sanctity of Christ. His sensitivity to the antagonistic powers of evil can be measured only by his sensitivity to the will of the Father.

Luke points out the sorry contrast between Christ and the apostles. The apostles did not pray nor did they endure an agony, but they were worn out with grief.

There are two other occasions during his passion when we hear Jesus' prayer, his prayer for his executioners and his prayer as he left this world and went to the Father. He prayed for those who were executing him. "Jesus said, 'Father, forgive them; they do not know what they are doing' " (Lk 23, 34). This prayer sums up the whole meaning of Jesus and his mission. He came to effect forgiveness of sins. His prayer for his executioners, which goes beyond those immediately present and extends to each one of us, expresses the meaning of his name, Jesus, which is Savior. His prayer and his actions were aspects of the single theme of his life, the salvation of mankind. It is a prayer which says all that he wanted to say throughout the whole of his life, a prayer which is given its efficacy in the very redemptive action which is taking place there on the cross.

His last words are the words of a Son who comes home to his Father. "Then Jesus gave a loud cry and said, 'Father, into thy hands I commit my spirit;' and with these words he died." There was an immediate effect, the prayer of praise coming from a gentile. "The centurion saw it all, and gave praise to God" (Lk 23, 46-47). His prayer is veiled prophecy of the prayer which will rise from the hearts and lips of other gentiles when they also see it all.

This last prayer of Jesus is the prayer of his passing over to the Father. In his first public appearance in the temple he had declared that he had to be busy with the affairs of his Father, or, what comes to the same thing, that he had to be occupied in his Father's house. This is the awareness which marked the consciousness of Jesus from beginning to end. It is this consciousness which is at the heart of the prayer life of Jesus. As the Father committed his affairs to Jesus, so now Jesus commits himself in the fulness of love to his Father.

The Gospel of Luke concludes with a description of the glorified Christ being taken up to heaven in the posture of prayer. "Then he led them out as far as Bethany, and blessed them with uplifted hands; and in the act of blessing he parted from them. And they returned to Jerusalem with great joy, and spent all their time in the temple praising God" (Lk 24, 50-53). As he left them, he blessed them. This blessing will have its fulfilment in the gift of the Holy Spirit. Their own reaction was not one of sorrow, as it was after the passion and death, but one of great joy, which expressed itself in prayer. They spent all of their time in the temple praising God for what he had accomplished in his Christ.

2. The Content of the Prayer of Christ in the Synoptics

When we try to form some idea of the content of the prayer of Jesus we realize immediately that it is not simply a matter of taking an inventory of various items which Jesus prayed for, and then cataloguing them. When we do get some inkling of the content of Jesus' prayer, these instances are more like "surfacings" of the prayer which lies deep beneath the surface. We can, so to speak, only make soundings of this prayer of Jesus. We cannot come up with a complete description of the content of the prayer of Jesus.

We mentioned at the beginning that a person's prayer life (as well as that of a people) is specified by the way in which he conceives his relationship to God. The prayer of Christ is, then, simply unique, because his relationship to God is unique. He is the only-begotten Son of the Father. The people of Israel prayed to the God who approached them in the covenant. The Christian prays in and through the Christ, who is God's definitive approach to men. But Christ prays as the very one in whom the Father approaches mankind. His prayer is not a response to a covenant. He is himself the embodiment of this covenant, and the one who invites others to enter into the covenant relationship.

We can come to some idea of the content of the prayer of Christ through appreciating as much as we can what Jesus loved, what he wanted, what he desired, what his concerns were. A person's prayer has to do with that which he wants the most, or loves the most. This means that Jesus' prayer must have the same content as that which is brought out by his name, Jesus, which means Savior. His whole meaning is to be Savior. His prayer must be an expression of that meaning.

His prayer then takes in all that is meant by salvation. This includes the persons to be saved and the means by which they will be saved. The discussions concerning the consciousness of Jesus and the kind of knowledge which Jesus had would be very much to the point here. To what extent is the prayer of Jesus merely global in its scope, unspecified, except for the goal which the Father wills, the salvation of mankind? To what extent is he praying for the realization of the design which he himself knows, or for the design which is known only to the Father? To what extent is he praying for individuals in their relationship to this design, as they are known to the Father, or only for the mass of mankind as it is known to an ordinary man? We feel that we are doing justice to the data of revelation only if we recognize in Christ a knowledge which takes his prayer out of the realm of the general, out of the category of genus or of species, and allows it to be specified by the particular means and the particular individuals as they are known by the Father.

As the definitive Word coming to mankind, he contains not simply a relationship to the means of salvation in general or to mankind in general. As the light which enlightens every man who comes into the world, there is also a knowledge which touches every man who comes into the world. As the one in whom God approaches man, each man, there is a knowledge of those whom he is approaching. Various theories may be devised to explain this kind of knowledge. But it seems that such knowledge must be postulated if we respect the fact that Jesus is not the Savior of mankind, but of individual men. His prayer is for the realization of God's design, not just any design, whatever it might be, but that design which he himself knows and wills.

We could approach the question of the content of Jesus' prayer in another way by saying he prayed for that which made a difference. In the phrase of Kierkegaard, "Truth is that which makes a difference." Christ prayed for those things which make a difference. That which made the greatest difference was the salvation of mankind. In the concrete, that which made the greatest difference was the relationship of each man to Christ.

What made a difference to Christ? We have an indication of this in the words which he spoke over Jerusalem. "O Jerusalem, Jerusalem, the city that murders the prophets and stones the messengers sent to her! How often have I longed to gather your children, as a hen gathers her brood under her wings; but you would not let me . . ." (Lk 13, 34). That which made the biggest difference was their response to him. More than any other person he felt their response to him. He rejoiced in their faith and was saddened by their rejection. He was saddened by the results of their rejection. The symbol of

God's presence among them, the temple, would be taken away from them. "Look, look! There is your temple, forsaken by God. And I tell you, you shall never see me until the time comes when you say, 'Blessings on him who comes in the name of the Lord' " (Lk 13, 35).

The content of the prayer of Jesus is suggested by the parables. In them he describes what he himself wants for men. He speaks of the sheep which is lost and of the joy which belongs to the shepherd when he finds it (Lk 15, 1-7), of the earnest seeking for one of the silver pieces and of the joy when it is found (Lk 15, 8-10), and of the joy of the Father who receives his son who was lost (Lk 25, 11-32).

We find an expression of the content of Jesus' prayer when he asks that the little ones come to him. "They even brought babies for him to touch; but when the disciples saw them they scolded them for it. But Jesus called for the children and said, 'Let the little ones come to me; do not try to stop them; for the kingdom of God belongs to such as these. I tell you that whoever does not accept the kingdom of God like a child will never enter it' " (Lk 18, 15-17). His prayer is that men be converted into little ones and come to him. The little ones are those who have become like himself, completely open to the will of the Father. His prayer is that men become converted into the simplicity of children, where their whole lives are simply the living out of the Father's will.

He also must have prayed that men would follow him in his own mode of life, a prayer which has given rise to a whole spectrum of different kinds of service which attempt to render present his own life of poverty, of celibacy, and of complete openness to the will of the Father. His desire for this type of service is seen in his invitation to the rich young man to follow Christ by selling all that he had, giving it to the poor, and putting all of his trust in the heavenly Father. The rich young man had asked, " 'Good master, what must I do to win eternal life?' "Jesus told him that he should keep the commandments. "The man answered, 'I have kept all these since I was a boy.' On hearing this Jesus said, 'There is still one thing lacking: sell everything you have and distribute to the poor, and you will have riches in heaven: and come, follow me.' At these words his heart sank; for he was a very rich man" (Lk 18, 18-23).

The prayer of Christ must have been directed to such individuals, not only that they might have life, but have it more abundantly, that they open themselves not only to Christ and to the Father's will in keeping the commandments, but also to the very means which Christ himself used, means which were sacrificial.

The following of Christ could involve not only the profession of poverty but also of celibacy for the kingdom of God. On the occasion when Jesus was speaking of the nature of marriage and its indissolubility, the disciples showed their reaction to this by saying, "If that is the position with husband and wife, it is better to refrain from marriage." Then Jesus replied, "That is something which not everyone can accept, but only those *for whom God has appointed it.* For while some are incapable of marriage because they were born so, or were made so by men, there are others who have themselves renounced marriage *for the sake of the kingdom of heaven.* Let those accept it who can" (Mt 19, 10-12).

All of the prayer of Jesus had to do with the kingdom of God, just as the whole meaning of his life was directed to the establishing of the kingdom of God. He spoke of the Father as appointing, as choosing some to mirror forth in their lives the nature of the kingdom of God in their celibacy. If Christ prayed for Peter, who was appointed by the Father for a particular role in the kingdom, he prayed also for those who were were appointed by the Father to bear witness to the kingdom in their lives of celibacy.

Again the content of Jesus' prayer is brought out when his presence in the house of Zacchaeus brings about the conversion of Zaccheus. "Jesus said to him, 'Salvation has come to this house today! — for this man too is a son of Abraham, and the Son of Man has come to seek and to save what is lost' " (Lk 19, 9-10). "To seek and to save" — this is the meaning of Jesus. His prayer could be expressed in no better way. It was a prayer of seeking and saving.

He must have prayed that men would worship the Father in a worship which was single-minded and free from all self-interest. The cleansing of the temple is simply an illustration of that which lay deep in his heart, and therefore an object of his prayer. "Then he went into the temple and began driving out the traders, with these words, 'Scripture says, "My house shall be a house of prayer"; but you have made it a robber's cave' " (Lk 19, 45-46).

The longing Jesus felt is brought out most especially in his desire to eat the passover with them before he suffered. "How I have longed to eat this passover with you before my death!" (Lk 22, 14-15). The gift of himself, the memorial of his own giving, must have had a privileged place in the consciousness of Jesus. What we long for the most is that which is most on our mind. It is that for which we pray. The gift of himself in the Eucharist was the subject of Jesus' meditation, the object of his longing, and the cause of his praise and thanksgiving to the Father.

We find another object of the prayer of Christ which he mentions explicitly. It is his prayer for Peter. "Simon, Simon! Satan, you must know, has got his wish to sift you all like wheat; but I have prayed for you, Simon, that your faith may not fail, and once you have recovered, you in your turn must strengthen your brothers" (Lk 22, 31-32). The object of Jesus' prayer is that his kingdom endure to the end of time. Peter is singled out in a special way as the object of Jesus' prayer to be the focal point of unity and strength in that kingdom.

The very center of all Jesus' prayer is brought out in the agony in the garden. It is a prayer that his Father's will be done. "Father, if it be thy will, take this cup away from me. Yet not my will but thine be done" (Lk 22, 42). This prayer is specifically sacrificial prayer when it is the Father's will that a person give himself *to another* by giving himself *for another*. It is not a prayer that God's will be done, as if this will were something abstract. It is a prayer professing complete openness to the will of the Father, even where this means a sacrifice of what we hold to be most precious.

Another object of the prayer of Christ is that men be led to repentance. This is what Jesus prayed for when he prayed for his executioners. "Father, forgive them; they

53

do not know what they are doing" (Lk 23,24).

His final prayer before his death is not one of petition or of praise or of thanks. It is the prayer in which time and eternity blend. It is a prayer which expresses the disposition of his whole life. His whole life had been lived in the Father's presence. The final act of his life is his irrevocable commitment to the Father. It is an act which is simply the follow-through of his whole life. "Father, into thy hands I commit my spirit" (Lk 23, 46). It is both an act of giving and also a prayer which expresses the gift. It is a prayer where the quiet note of victory is already present. He had told his mother and father when they were searching for him, "Did you not know that I was bound to be in my Father's house?" (Lk 2, 49). All of his activity, all of his consciousness, was in his Father's house. Now he quietly commits himself with the fulness of trust into the hands of the Father. It is the prayer of Jesus' passover.

We have further indication of the content of Jesus' prayer in the description of the resurrection appearances where Jesus opened the minds of the disciples to understand what was said of him. His role, however, is changed. He not only explains the Scripture. Now he has power to open their minds to understand the Scripture. Those very mysteries contained in Scripture must have formed the subject matter of Jesus' own prayerful meditation.

We read how he met the disciples on their way to Emmaus. "Then he began with Moses and all the prophets, and explained to them the passages which referred to himself in every part of Scripture" (Lk 24, 27). Later when he appeared to the Eleven, "He said to them, 'This is what I meant by saying, while I was still with you, that everything written about me in the Law of Moses and in the prophets and psalms was bound to be fulfilled.' Then he opened their minds to understand the Scriptures. 'This,' he said, 'is what is written: that the Messiash is to suffer death and to rise from the dead on the third day, and that in his name repentance bringing the forgiveness of sins is to be proclaimed to all nations. Begin from Jerusalem: it is you who are the witnesses to all this. And mark this: I am sending you my Father's promised gift; so stay here in this city until you are armed with the power from above' " (Lk 24, 44-49). Those passages, then, which referred to him in every part of Scripture must have formed the subject of Jesus' meditation.

We have further indication of the object of Jesus' prayer. If all of the gifts which came from the Father came because of Jesus' prayer, the gift which must have been the chief object was the gift of gifts, the Holy Spirit, in whom all the other gifts are contained.

The final gesture of Christ on earth is, as we saw an act of blessing. Through this gesture he shows forth his whole meaning. He leaves his disciples while he blesses them, with uplifted hands. This blessing is a prayer that they, together with all mankind, may be blessed with the gifts which Jesus has gained for them through his redemptive life. He ascends into heaven in the posture of prayer and with a prayer on his lips. This is the posture which he maintains until his second coming. It is a posture of prayer that the blessings of the redemption be fully bestowed through the gift of the Spirit.

We have seen that the content of the prayer of Christ is simply the conscious expression of what Christ is, of his identify as Savior. If we asked what the central element was in all the prayer of Jesus, whether in the prayer of petition, or of praise, or of thanksgiving, we would have to say that it is the prayer that the will of God be done. His life found its meaning in being the perfect living out of the will of the Father. All of his prayer is related to this; all of the various forms which this prayer can take are found in his prayer with the one exception of the prayer of sorrow or repentance. This shows how perfectly his prayer is the expression of his life, in perfect conformity with the will of the Father.

When the will of the Father is experienced in terms of grace and gift, then it causes Jesus to exult, and his prayer takes the form of praise (Lk 10, 21). When the will of God is seen as the will for men's salvation, then the prayer of Christ takes the form of petition. When the will of God is seen in terms of the establishing of the kingdom, then Christ prays for those means which have to do with the kingdom—the Eucharist, which is the perpetuation of his doing-the-will-of-the-Father, the choice of the apostles, the special commission to Peter, the perseverance of Peter in his vocation. When Jesus sees the will of the Father fulfilled, then there is joy, as in the case of the repentant sinner. When the will of the Father asks that Jesus enter into the role of the Suffering Servant and offer himself sacrificially for mankind, then the prayer of Christ becomes sacrificial prayer, the will to open himself to the Father even though it means the sacrifice of himself. This is the prayer of the agony. Throughout the prayer of Jesus is that the will of the Father be done. The first three petitions of the "Lord's prayer" truly echo the prayer of the Lord, that the name of the Father be hallowed, that his kingdom come, and that his will be done. His prayer expressed in desire that which his life expressed in fact — the perfect living out of the will of the Father.

3. The Prayer Of Christ In The Gospel Of St. John

One could expect that the prayer of Jesus as described in the Fourth Gospel would have the same characteristics which mark off this gospel from the synoptics. In the other gospels, for one thing, there is the constant awareness of the movement of time and of concrete details. Jesus moves and lives in the other gospels in much the same way as any other figure, at least from an external point of view. But the Fourth Gospel is rather a description of presence than of movement. The presence of Jesus embodies the "I am" of God, the very Name and meaning of Yahweh. His appearance there takes on the nature of Greek eikon, where the inner meaning is allowed to shape the outer expression.

This is not to deny that there is movement and development in the Fourth Gospel, or to infer that Jesus is simply an inert figure being carried along across a stage of living human beings. But the perspective from which John writes is that of one who has experienced and is experiencing the glorified Christ in his church through the activity of the Spirit. The Spirit of the glorified Christ gives the set to the descriptions in the Fourth Gospel.

These characteristics are also seen in the prayer of Christ as it is described in the Fourth Gospel. The prayer of the synoptics is directed to the founding of the kingdom and to all of the gifts necessary for the perpetuation of the kingdom. In the Fourth Gospel, however, the prayer of Jesus takes place from within his presence in the kingdom. This is typical of the tone of the whole gospel. It is a gospel of the presence of Jesus in the church, through the gift of his Spirit. But this presence is not simply a being-there. It is a consecrating presence. The whole of John's gospel is a description of the consecrating presence of Jesus. First of all there is the description of the consecration of Jesus himself, who becomes the temple, and through him all of the feasts and institutions of the people of Israel are consecrated and given a new meaning. There are in addition new rites of consecration, baptism and the Eucharist, to take the place of the old rites.

This progressive consecration is the object of Jesus' prayer and of all his activity. As he says, "For their sake do I consecrate myself, that they too may be consecrated by the truth" (Jn 17, 19). It is a consecration which, first of all, is manifested progressively in his own life to the point where he offers himself as the Lamb of God. The climax of Jesus' own consecration is at the same time the initiation of man's. He says "It is finished" (Jn 19, 30), and bows his head and gives over the Spirit. The means by which men are consecrated are symbolized in the water and the blood which flowed from his pierced side. They become consecrating or sanctifying because he gives over his Spirit to enliven them and make them sacramental means of sanctification.

THE PRAYER OF CHRIST IN THE GOSPEL OF ST. JOHN

With those remarks serving as an introduction we can turn directly to the prayer of Christ in the Fourth Gospel. There are, in fact, only a few examples of the prayer of Christ there, apart from the prayer at the Last Supper. When he multiplies the loaves, he is described as giving thanks (Jn 6, 11). At the raising of Lazarus, he prayed. "Then Jesus looked upwards and said, "Father, I thank thee: thou hast heard me. I knew already that thou always hearest me, but I spoke for the sake of the people standing round, that they might believe that thou didst send me.' " (Jn 11, 41-42). This gives an insight into the prayer of Jesus. His prayer is always heard by the Father. It is the prayer of a Son, and his Father always hears his prayer. And yet being a faithful Son he prays for what his Father wills.

We have another example of the prayer of Jesus when the Greeks who had come to the feast come to the disciples and ask to see Jesus. The whole passage is concerned with the salvation of the Gentiles. Their presence, and their desire to see him, place him as it were by anticipation in the hour of his passion. He says, " 'Now my soul is in turmoil, and what am I to say? Father, save me from this hour? No, it was for this that I came to this hour. Father, glorify thy name.' A voice sounded from heaven: 'I have glorified it, and I will glorify it again' " (Jn 12, 27-28). This glory, Jesus goes on to say, comes from overcoming the powers of evil, and in drawing all men to himself. " 'Now is the hour of judgment for this world; now shall the Prince of this world be driven out. And I shall draw all men to myself, when I am lifted up from the earth.' This he said to indicate the kind of death he was to die" (Jn 12, 31-33).

We find here the basic prayer of Jesus, that his Father be glorified. The glory of the Father, the brightness of his presence, will come at the hour of Jesus, which is at one and the same time the period of darkness and of glory.

These are the only examples of the prayer of Jesus in the Fourth Gospel. The various occasions which are singled out in the synoptics are not mentioned by John. Could we suggest a reason for this?

We have already suggested that this fits in with the whole pattern of John's gospel, where the emphasis is on the consecrating presence of Jesus through the gift of his Spirit. But we do see a certain progression in John's vision over what we find in the synoptics, just as we see a certain progression in Luke's description of the prayer of Jesus over that of Mark's gospel. In Mark we saw that Jesus' activity was punctuated by prayer at critical moments in the establishing of the kingdom. In Luke we have the impression that the prayer of Jesus is the constant atmosphere in which he lives. His activity flows from, and is in continuity with his prayer. In John there seems to be a further development. There is simply the atmosphere of communion of life and love. We could say that it is a communion of uninterrupted vision and of love, where the prayer of petition has become the prayer of union.

This comes from the intimate union of the Father and the Son. The Son is also the point of union or communion of the Father with the world. He is the one on whom they will see heaven opened and the angels ascending and descending (Jn 1, 51). There are many references to this union of Christ with the Father, both in terms of mutual indwelling, and in terms of Jesus' doing the will of the Father. "It is meat and drink for me to do the will of him who sent me until I have finished his work" (Jn 4, 34). "What the Father does, the Son does" (Jn 5, 19). "For as the Father has life—giving power in himself, so has the Son, by the Father's gift" (Jn 5, 26). "He who sent me is present with me, and has not left me alone; for I always do what is acceptable to him" (Jn 8, 29). "My Father and I are one" (Jn 10, 30). "Do you not believe that I am in the Father, and the Father in me? I am not myself the source of the words I speak to you: it is the Father who dwells in me doing his own work. Believe me when I say that I am in the Father and the Father in me" (Jn 14, 10-11). "May they all be one: as thou, Father, are in me, and I in thee" (Jn 17, 21).

This union of Jesus with the Father means that the Son is the mediator of the word of the Father to men. "What the Father has said to me, therefore—that is what I speak" (Jn 12, 50). "I have called you friends, because I have disclosed to you everything that I heard from my Father" (Jn 15, 15). "No one ever went up to heaven except the one who came down from heaven, the Son of Man whose home is in heaven" (Jn 3, 13). Only the one who is in heaven can bring heavenly gifts to those on earth.

This then is the nature of Jesus' prayer. It is a prayer of union which is deep and still, but it overflows into prayer for men, to draw then into this union with the Father. He is one with the Father and also one with mankind. He is one with mankind in order to make them one with himself in his union with the Father.

This union is the object of what has been called his High Priestly Prayer in chapter seventeen, to which we now turn our attention.

The prayer is divided into three parts. Each part is a prayer for life, but for that life which comes from union with the Son and through him with the Father. In the first part Jesus prays that the life which he has with the Father from all eternity be now manifested in his body. This glory cannot be separated from the flesh of all those who belong to him, that is, those who are described as the branches on the vine (Jn 15, 1-8). Jesus has been given authority over all mankind for this one purpose, to bring them eternal life. "For thou hast made him sovereign over all mankind to give eternal life to all whom thou hast given him" (Jn 17, 2). His own glory is achieved when this gift of eternal life is manifested among those who accept him through their faith.

In the second part of the prayer he prays for the disciples who were given him by the Father. The purpose of his prayer is summed up in one sentence: "Holy Father keep them true to thy name, thy gift to me, that they may be one, as we are one" (Jn 17, 11). Being true to his name means that they will have the joy which belongs to Christ himself, who always did the will of the Father and was loyal to his name. It also involves suffering. They will suffer the hatred of the world because of their loyalty to the truth. "The world has nothing but hatred for them, because they do not belong to the world, as I, too, do not belong to the world" (Jn 17, 14). He puts the same petition in a negative way, that they be preserved from evil: "I pray thee, not to take them out of the world, but to keep them from the evil one. They are strangers in the world, as I am" (Jn 17,

15). The petition that they remain faithful is then put in the strongest possible form, that they be consecrated, dedicated entirely to the truth. "Consecrate them by the truth; thy word is truth. As thou hast sent me into the world, I have sent them into the world, and for their sake I consecrate myself, that they too may be consecrated by the truth" (Jn 17, 18-20). The word "truth" as used here is not an abstraction. To explain it John wrote the gospel. It is the person of Christ in the fullness of his meaning, with his relationship to the Father, his relationship to men. It takes in the whole economy of the redemption as this economy is brought to fruition in Christ.

In the third place Jesus prays for those who will believe in him through the words of the Apostles. Again his prayer has one purpose: that the oneness which he has with the Father be shared with those who believe in him, and finally that this oneness be complete, to the point that where Jesus is, there also those who believe in him may be. "But it is not for these alone that I pray, but for those also who through their words put their faith in me; may they be one: as thou, Father, art in me, and I in thee, so also may they be one in us....I in them and thou in me, may they be perfectly one....Father, I desire that these men, who are thy gift to me, may be with me where I am, so that they may look upon my glory, which thou hast given me because thou didst love me before the world began....I made thy name known to them, and will make it known, so that the love thou hadst for me may be in them, and I may be in them" (Jn 17, 20-26).

We see then, the nature of the prayer of Jesus in the Gospel of St. John. It flows from uninterrupted union with the Father. It is the Father's good pleasure that this union be opened in order to draw men into this love relationship. This takes place through the redemptive life of Christ. It is also the object of his prayer, which itself is part of his redemptive life. His prayer is not tangential to the rest of his life. It is safe to say that he could not have been Jesus, Savior, unless he prayed for that which he accomplished, that is, unless he expressed in the deepest desire of his heart that which he accomplished through his actions. His prayer at the Last Supper is like the words of consecration spoken over himself, and over all those who would believe in him. The transubstantiation does not take place all at once in those who believe in him. But it will be completed when his prayer is completely answered, "That the love thou hadst for me may be in them, and I may be in them" (Jn 17, 26).

4. The Prayer Of Christ In The Epistle To The Hebrews

Both the Gospel of John and the Epistle to the Hebrews emphasize the intercessory nature of Christ's prayer. In John the intercessory power comes from the communion which Jesus has with the Father, an uninterrupted awareness of the presence of the Father. In Hebrews it comes from the communion which Jesus has with men. He can pray for us because he has shared our experience. In both cases, of course, there is the communion of Christ with God and man, but there is a different emphasis in each case.

In Hebrews the unique nature of the intercessory power of Christ comes from his uniqueness as priest. This is based in the first place on the fact that he is the Son of God. "But in this final age he has spoken to us in the Son whom he has made heir to the whole universe, and through whom he created all orders of existence; the Son who is the effulgence of God's splendor and the stamp of God's very being, and sustains the universe by his word of power" (Heb 1, 2-3).

This Son is very God. "Thy throne, O God, is forever and ever," are the words which are used to describe him (Heb 1, 8). He is the Lord of all the world. Everything is subject to him. "For in subjecting all things to him, he left nothing that is not subject" (Heb 1, 8). These thoughts could be said to be reminiscent of John's own thinking. Then we come to the particular emphasis of Hebrews. How was everything made subject to him? Because of his experience of human suffering and death. "In Jesus, however, we do see one who for a short while was made lower than the angels, crowned now with glory and honor because he suffered death, so that, by God's gracious will, in tasting death, he should stand for us all" (Heb 2, 9).

Jesus became our high priest, and enjoys the unique role of intercessor because of his identification with man. "It was clearly fitting that God for whom and through whom all things exist should, in bringing many sons to glory, make the leader who delivers them perfect through sufferings. For a consecrating priest and those whom he consecrates are all of one stock; and that is why the Son does not shrink from calling men his brothers, when he says, 'I will proclaim thy name to my brothers; in full assembly I will sing thy praise.' Again, 'I will keep my trust fixed on him'; and again, 'Here am I, and the children whom God has given me.' The children of a family share the same flesh and blood; and so he too shared ours, so that through death he might break the power of him who had death at his command, that is, the devil; and might liberate those who through fear of death, had all their lifetime been in servitude. It is not angels, mark you, that he takes to himself, but the sons of Abraham. And therefore he had to be made like these brothers of his in every way, so that he might be merciful and faithful as their high priest before God to expiate the sins of the people. For since he himself passed through the test of suffering, he is able to help those who are meeting their test now" (Heb 2, 10-18).

In this way Jesus is our mediator in a unique way. He is both the Son of the Father, and the brother of men. His mediatorship differs from that, for example, of Moses. Moses was a mediator as a servant in God's household, but Christ is the Son set over the household. "Moses, then, was faithful as a servitor in God's whole household; his task was to bear witness to the words that God would speak; but Christ is faithful as a Son, set over his household. And we are that household of his" (Heb 3, 5-6).

The theme that Christ is our priest because he identified himself with us recurs over and over again. "For ours is not a high priest unable to symphathize with our weaknesses, but one who, because of his likeness to us, has been tested in every way, only without sin. Let us therefore boldly approach the throne of our gracious God, where we may receive mercy and in his grace find timely help" (Heb 4, 15-16). "In the days of his earthly life he offered up prayers and petitions, with loud cries and tears, to God who was able to deliver him from the grave. Because of his humble submission his prayer was heard: Son though he was, he learned obedience in the school of suffering, and, once perfected, became the source of eternal salvation for all who obey him, named by God high priest in the succession of Melchizedek" (Heb 5, 7-10).

Another characteristic of the priesthood of Christ is that it is perpetual. His priesthood endures for all eternity. "The priesthood which Jesus holds is perpetual, because he remains forever. That is why he is also able to save absolutely those who approach God through him; he is always living to plead on their behalf" (Heb 7,24-25). The prayer of Christ is based on his perpetual priesthood. This means that his prayer is not intermittent. His intercession continues without the interruptions that belong to time. The rhythm of time has given way to that of eternity, so that he can become our full-time intercessor with the Father.

The sacrifice which he offered for us is that which fits his priesthood. It is the sacrifice of one who is the Son of the Father, and therefore, without sin; at the same time the sacrifice of one who identified himself with us in our sinful condition, without however taking on our own alienation from the Father, which of course would contradict his very nature as Son of the Father. "Such a high priest does indeed fit our condition—devout, guileless, undefiled, separated from sinners, raised high above the heavens. He has no need to offer sacrifices daily, as the high priests do, first for his own sins and then for those of the people; for this he did once and for all when he offered up himself. The high priests made by the Law are men in all their frailty; but the priest appointed by the word of the oath which supersedes the Law is the Son, made perfect now and forever" (Heb 7, 26-28).

Christ is described as praying to the Father at the very moment of his coming into the world. "That is why, at his coming into the world, he says, 'Sacrifice and offering thou didst not desire, but thou hast prepared a body for me. Whole-offerings and sin-offerings thou didst not delight in. Then I said, "Here am I: as it

is written of me in the scroll, I have come, O God, to do
thy will." ' First he says, 'Sacrifices and offerings,
whole-offerings and sin-offerings, thou didst not desire
nor delight in'—although the Law prescribes them—and
then he says, 'I have come to do thy will.' He thus
annuls the former to establish the latter. And it is by the
will of God that we have been consecrated, through the
offering of the body of Jesus Christ once and for all"
(Heb 10, 5-10).

Christ is, then, the unique intercessor. For this reason
we can approach God with confidence. Cleansed with
his blood, sprinkled with the waters of baptism, with
hearts filled with faith, we can approach God with confidence through the one who is interceding for us. "So
now, my friends, the blood of Jesus makes us free to
enter boldly into the sanctuary by the new, living way
which he has opened for us through the curtain, the way
of his flesh. We have, moreover, a great priest set over
the household of God; so let us make our approach in
sincerity of heart and full assurance of faith, our guilty
hearts sprinkled clean, our bodies washed with pure
water. Let us be firm and unswerving in the confession
of our hope, for the Giver of the promise may be
trusted" (Heb 10, 19-24). Because Christ continues to
exercise his priesthood for us we have access to the
Father through him. This means that the heavens are
constantly opened to the Christian. They did not close
behind Jesus after his entrance to the Father. Because
Jesus is constantly interceding for us the way is constantly opened for us to the Father.

The fact that Jesus is the undying mediator puts us in
the presence not only of the Father but in the presence

of the whole assembly of those who belong to the heavenly court. "You stand before Mount Zion and the city of the living God, heavenly Jerusalem, before myriads of angels, the full concourse and assembly of the first-born citizens of heaven, and God the judge of all, and the spirits of good men made perfect, and Jesus the mediator of a new covenant, whose sprinkled blood has better things to tell than the blood of Abel" (Heb 13, 15).

Our own prayer should be offered through our great high priest and intercessor, Jesus. "Through Jesus, then, let us continually offer up to God the sacrifice of praise, that is, the tribute of lips which acknowledge his name, and never forget to show kindness and to share what you have with others; for such are the sacrifices which God approves" (Heb 13, 15).

What then can we say about the nature of Christ's prayer as we find it described in Hebrews? First of all the very basis of his prayer lies in the fact that his existence lies completely on the side of God, as Son and as Lord, and also completely on the side of man, in that he identified himself with us in everything except sin. Hebrews brings out both aspects of the meaning of Christ, but it emphasizes the identity he has with the flesh of mankind.

As his prayer is described in Hebrews, there are no references to special moments in the life of Christ when he prayed (as we find in the synoptics). Rather the individual moments are, as it were, universalized to cover the whole life of Christ. For example, the prayer of the agony is universalized to cover his whole life. "In the days of his earthly life he offered up prayers and petitions, with loud cries and tears, to God who was able to deliver him from the grave" (Heb 5, 7). His prayer was anguished prayer, but it was efficacious because he was doing the will of the Father. He was not delivered from death, but delivered from the grave, through the resurrection. Here the resurrection is seen as a direct answer to the prayer of Christ. In a similar way he is described as praying when he came into the world. His prayer in the words of Psalm 40 declares his perfect openness to the will of the Father.

His prayer for others is the prayer of intercession. His intercession is related to his priesthood, which endures forever. The effects of his priesthood on earth are carried over into heaven where he continues to exercise his priesthood through intercession. "That is why he is also able to save absolutely those who approach God through him; he is always living to plead on their behalf" (Heb 7, 25). The fruits of his priesthood are not stored away some place in the past. All of his priestly life is caught up here and now in the climax of that priestly life. He is freed from the limitations of time so that he can apply the effects of his priesthood to those who are within time. We who are still within the confines of time with all of its weaknesses and uncertainties have confidence in the fact that there is one of us always standing before the face of the Father interceding for his brothers. He can pray for our needs, because he more than any other has experienced the totality of those needs—the need, first of all, at the very root of our being for life everlasting, and all of our other needs as well. He knows how much we need to be helped by his prayer because he has also experienced our helplessness in taking on himself our own suffering and death.

PART II. THE PRAYER OF THE CHRISTIAN

The prayer of the Christian has a distinctiveness to it which marks it off from all other prayer. The words which are used may be the same but there is a completely distinctive mark to Christian prayer. The basic distinction is that it is the prayer of a son. Through the life of grace one takes on a new mode of existence. His actions speak forth sonship (or at least they should). His prayer also speaks forth sonship. His prayer is different not only because he has new information about God, or about his own needs. His prayer is different because he is now praying from *within* a relationship, from within the relationship that the Son has to the Father. His own words to the Father begin to share in Christ's words to the Father. His whole being is drawn into this relationship. His prayer shares in this new life and expresses the new life. There is a new energy at the source of his prayer life. That energy is the Spirit who is given by Christ. The Spirit is constantly moving the Christian to speak forth the whole of Christ: in all of his actions, including his prayer, to speak his relationship to the Father.

We are considering here the prayer of the Christian, that is, of one who has been baptized, has entered into the fellowship of Christ through the sacraments, and whose life is nourished through the sacraments. It is true that wherever there is an action which is graced, there is the prayer of sonship, even if a person has not entered into the sacramental fellowship of Christ. Grace always relates us to the Son and through him to the Father, and a prayer which comes forth from a life which is graced is always the prayer of sonship. But in our treatment we are not considering such cases. When the New Testament speaks of the new fellowship that we call the church it is the fellowship that comes through the sacraments. Though there can be genuine prayer outside of this sacramental fellowship, such prayer cannot really exist without some relationship to this fellowship. The prayer of sonship wherever it is found must be rooted in or related to the sacramental union of men with Christ in the church. The words which we speak to God in prayer, when they really share in the speaking of Christ to the Father, must find their life-giving impulse in the form in which the Word of God has been given to mankind in a final, definitive way: in the church.

For the sake of convenience we shall study the prayer of the Christian by commenting on the various books of the New Testament which tell us something about prayer. We shall begin with the synoptics, concentrating mainly on the Gospel of Luke, supplementing this where necessary with what is found in Matthew and Mark. We shall go on then to the Gospel of John, and the other books of the New Testament.

1. The Prayer of the Christian in the Synoptics

St. Luke shows a special interest in prayer. His gospel begins with a description of the Jewish people at prayer and ends with the description of Christ ascending into heaven while praying and tells us that the disciples spent all of their time in the temple in prayer. Then his narration in the Acts takes up where he left off in his Gospel, with a description of the community at prayer. "All those were constantly at prayer together, and with them a group of women, including Mary the mother of Jesus, and his brothers" (Ac 1, 14).

The first chapters of the Gospel of Luke are filled with examples of prayer. There are the hymns of Mary and Zechariah which are filled with the joy that belonged to the messianic age. There is the angelic song which the heavenly host sang at the coming of the Messiah. "Glory to God in the highest heaven, and peace to men who enjoy his favor" (Lk 2, 14). There is Simeon's prayerful *"Nunc dimittis,"* which is a prayer of trust in God's loving providence. In the coming of the Messiah he sees the fulfilment of God's promise to himself, to the people of Israel, and to all of the nations. He is like the watchman in the tower, who retires when the sun begins to rise. There is quiet trust in God's power to bring his promises to fruition.

Each of these prayers would merit detailed consideration. But that would take us beyond the scope of our study. These prayers have become part of the Christian treasury of prayer. They are the prayers evoked when salvation appears on the horizon. But beautiful and expressive as they are, they still do not have the dimension that prayer will have, once the sun has run its course. When that takes place prayer is changed, just as all of our actions are changed. Our prayer takes place not only with Christ before our eyes as Savior, but our prayer, as all of our actions, takes place in Christ, through the gift of his Spirit.

The first direct reference to Christian prayer occurs in the context of our relationship to those who harm us. "Love your enemies; do good to those who hate you; bless those who curse you; *pray* for those who treat you spitefully" (Lk 6, 28). Christ is calling the Christian to a new mode of love. Christian prayer must be a practical expression of this new mode of love. "If you love only those who love you, what credit is that to you . . . But you must love your enemies" (Lk 6, 32-35). Love for our enemies must show itself in prayer for them.

Christian prayer is directed to the realization of Christ's kingdom. He exhorts his disciples to pray that the Father send laborers into the harvest. "He said to them, 'The crop is heavy, but laborers are scarce; you must therefore beg the owner to send laborers to harvest his crop' " (Lk 10, 2). We find here a note which characterizes Christian prayer. The kingdom of God is a work which depends on the prayer of the Christian. The kingdom is a collaborative work. This is a note which is distinctive of the New Testament. In the Old Testament there is prayer that God send his Anointed to bring the kingdom of God into existence. We do not, however, find prayer that God send co-workers to the people of Israel. He does in fact send the prophets, but we find no prayer for them among the people of Israel. We have the impression that God's kingdom comes from above, through his vertical action in time. But in the New Testament, though the kingdom comes from above it also comes from below, along the horizontal line of man's cooperation. One way in which he cooperates is through his prayer for the laborors who are needed for the kingdom. As the laborors are truly needed, and not just accessory, so the prayer of the Christian is truly needed. This is a conviction which, as we shall see, runs through the epistles of St. Paul. The spread of the kingdom depends on the prayers of Christians.

In the passage quoted above it is likely that the "Lord of the harvest" is Christ himself. It is a passage within the context of the missionary journey of the disciples. It begins, "After this the Lord appointed seventy-two others and sent them out ahead of him, in pairs, to all the towns and places he himself was to visit" (Lk 10, 1). The missionary work was a work of collaboration with him. They would go first; he would come after them. This missionary activity is symbolic of the activity which will take place when Jesus is exalted as Lord at the right hand of the Father after his ascension. But even though the Lord is in heaven and his missionaries on earth, the work is still a work of collaboration. The Lord makes himself present in and through his workers.

But part of their work is their prayer to the one who

reigns as Lord, to send more workers into the harvest. In this way Christian prayer takes on a particularly sacramental characteristic. If we think of sacrament in a wide sense as those actions of men which bring to bear the fulness of Christ to their fellowmen, then prayer, Christian prayer, is sacramental. It is not simply looking to the future. It is rooted in the past, especially in the redemptive act of Christ. It is prayer which releases that which is in Christ and in this way builds up the kingdom in time, through human instrumentality. All Christian prayer, when it is directed to building up the kingdom, is sacramental, asking that the fulness which is in Christ be given to mankind. Putting it in another way, it is prayer that the world be released and allowed to come to Christ. As Christ said, "When I am lifted up from the earth I shall draw all men to myself" (Jn 12, 32). The work of Christian prayer, part of Christian missionary work, is to release men that they can be drawn to Christ.

In chapter eleven we find Jesus' explicit teaching on prayer. "Once in a certain place, Jesus was at prayer. When he ceased, one of his disciples said, 'Lord, teach us to pray, as John taught his disciples.' He answered, "When you pray, say: Father, thy name be hallowed; thy kingdom come; give us each day our daily bread. And forgive us our sins, for we too forgive all who have done us wrong. And lead us not into temptation' " (Lk 11, 1-4).

The words of Jesus were given to us as a model form of prayer. They were not given to be adhered to exactly, as we can see from the differences in Luke's version as compared with that of Matthew. Matthew's text, which appears to be the more ancient, has seven petitions; Luke's only five. The formulation as we have it in Luke is perhaps the result of liturgical use in the early Christian community.

We should not think that the disciples asked to be taught to pray as if they had not been praying and now wanted to learn how to pray. As faithful Jews they prayed in the synagogue and said the daily prayers prescribed for the Jews. What they wanted to learn was to pray as Jesus prayed. They were asking for more than a lesson. They were seeking for the revelation of the inner meaning of Jesus. Their desire was partially motivated by what they witnessed in the master-disciple relationship between John and his disciples. John taught his disciples to pray; since Jesus was their master, he should teach them how to pray. But beyond that there must have been the attraction that came from the mystery of Jesus' own life of prayer. In giving them this prayer he revealed his own inner life, and at the same time his realization of the needs of men.

A basic orientation forms the axis of this prayer. From it all of the petitions radiate. It is the relationship of the Christian to the Father. This is to be understood in a specifically Christian sense, not in the sense of the Fatherhood of God as we could know him from reason or from the Old Testament. The prayer is directed to the Father of our Lord Jesus Christ, and therefore to our Father because of our relationship to Christ. Taken by themselves the individual petitions could be said by any one who worshipped the true God in the Old Covenant. The individual petitions could be paraphrased from the psalms. But the Our Father is specifically a Christian prayer. There is the realization that all of the petitions are implicitly terminated with the expression which we find so often in St. Paul, "through Jesus Christ." "Thy name be hallowed—through Jesus Christ; thy Kingdom come—through Jesus Christ; thy will be done—through Jesus Christ." Christian prayer is such because it takes place in and through Christ.

This prayer has always played a large part in the liturgical and devotional life of the Christian. The commentaries on it are numerous. Tertullian called it the epitome of the whole Gospel. St. Augustine spoke of it as the source of all other prayers. Through commentaries and special treatises it became the textbook for Christian prayer. Among others we have the commentaries of Tertullian, Origen, Cyprian, Augustine, St. Thomas Aquinas, and St. Teresa of Avila. Since we cannot do justice to the prayer itself, we shall content ourselves with referring to these commentaries as helps to appreciate its richness.

Christian prayer, then, is always in the presence of the Father, for him to see and for him to hear. He hears as a Father hears, not the words, whether they be sophisticated or not, but the heart behind the words. *He* knows our heart before we speak. But *we* do not know our heart before we speak. In our prayer we let our heart speak to the Father, and he will hear.

Immediately following the version of the Lord's Prayer in Luke, Jesus makes use of two comparisons to motivate men to pray with perseverance. In order to show the relationship of the Christian to his heavenly Father, he draws the analogy of one friend helping another, and of a father helping his child. They are arguments *a fortiori*. If those who are so imperfect listen to persevering prayer, then how much more will our heavenly Father listen to us and give us the most precious of all gifts, his Holy Spirit.

"Suppose one of you has a friend who comes to him in the middle of the night and says, 'My friend, lend me three loaves, for a friend of mine on a journey has turned up at my house, and I have nothing to offer him.' And he replies from inside, 'Do not bother me. The door is shut for the night; my children and I have gone to bed; and I cannot get up and give you what you want.' I tell you that even if he will not provide for him out of friendship, the very shamelessness of the request will make him get up and give him all he needs. And I say to you, ask, and you will receive; seek, and you will find; knock, and the door will be opened. For everyone who asks receives, he who seeks finds, and to him who knocks the door will be opened. Is there a father among you who will offer his son a snake when he asks for fish, or a scorpion when he asks for an egg? If you, then, bad as you are, know how to give your children what is good for them, how much more will the heavenly Father give the Holy Spirit to those who ask him!" (Lk 11, 5-13).

The basic lesson is that a friend, if he is a true friend, will fulfill the needs of his friend, even though it be inconvenient to do so at the time. He will, as the gospel account says, give him *all that he needs,* not only that which he asked for. The person in the story only wanted to borrow three loaves. But his friend gives him all that he needs, not only lends him the loaves. A father is aware of the needs that his son has for food and gives him what is necessary to fulfill these needs. Even more, God our heavenly Father knows our needs and fulfills them when we ask. Our basic need is for the gift of the Spirit. Perhaps the lesser needs are not satisfied in our prayer, but the greater need, to live through the gift of the Spirit, is always satisfied when we approach God in prayer.

Yet even before we can receive the gift of the Spirit there is another need which has to be filled. It is the need for forgiveness. In the parable of the Prodigal Son we have the moving account of the desire of the Father to forgive those who ask for forgiveness. The parable tells the story of the son who left his father, lived a sinful life, and then petitioned his father to be accepted back into the house, not as a son but as a servant. We read how the son finally made up his mind to return, and set out for his father's house. "But while he was a long way off his father saw him, and his heart went out to him. He ran to meet him, flung his arms round him, and kissed him" (Lk 15, 20). In the form of a parable we have a description of the life of each man and the workings of grace in his heart. His prayer for forgiveness comes from himself but also is anticipated by the Father. It is the father's presence at work even when the son is far away, the father's presence drawing him, attracting his freedom, to resolve to return. It is the father who runs out to meet the son even before he gets to the house. He not only welcomes the son with courtesy but is overjoyed with his return. Throughout it is the father's presence which is eliciting, attracting, embracing. It is in fact in *forgiving* that he shows himself more of a father than in giving. To forgive draws upon the deepest power of the heart to give. It is an act which is not only an act of love, but an act of love which is intense enough to consume and overcome resistance and rejection. It is like a medicine which not only has the power to prevent death, but even the power to overcome death, and restore life.

Prayer for forgiveness will always be part of Christian prayer. Before we can enjoy any other gift of God we have to be forgiven and stand in his presence. In the Christian community there is the realization that the Father has come to us, put his arms about us, kissed us. But this has all happened in his Son. Forgiveness is received through the embrace of the Son. Perhaps we have lost the sense of the need for forgiveness. To the extent that this is lost we also have lost the gospel. We do not understand the love of the Father who loved us while we were yet sinners (Rm 5, 8). The world has become "healthy" and does not need the physician, when the need for forgiveness is no longer realized.

There is only one unanswered prayer described in the gospel. It is the prayer of the rich man who died and was buried in hell. "He looked up, and there, far away, was Abraham with Lazarus close beside him. 'Abraham, my father,' he called out, 'take pity on me! Send Lazarus to dip the tip of his finger in water to cool my tongue, for I am in agony in this fire.' 'My son,' Abraham replied 'remember that during your life good things came your way, just as bad things came the way of Lazarus. Now he is being comforted here while you are in agony. But that is not all: between us and you a great gulf has been fixed, to stop anyone, if he wanted to, crossing from our side to yours, and to stop any crossing from your side to ours' " (Lk 16, 23-26). When the rich man asks for someone to be sent to warn his brothers about the place of torment, he is told that if his brothers do not believe Moses and the prophets they will not believe the word of someone who rose from the dead.

Though it is not the primary purpose of this parable to teach a lesson about prayer, it does serve to bring home to us that the time will come when prayer can no longer be heard. This is hell, the situation where prayer can no longer be heard. Prayer becomes the echo of what might have been but can never be. It becomes part of the contradiction that makes hell what it is.

There are several passages in Mark, not found in Luke, which bring out other aspects of prayer. In one of them a father brought his son to the disciples to be cured of the evil spirit which possessed him. The disciples were unable to cast out this spirit. Then Jesus, after eliciting faith from the father, cast out the spirit. After this happened, we read, "When he had gone indoors his disciples asked him privately, 'Why were we unable to cast it out? 'This is the kind' he answered, 'that can be driven out only by prayer' " (Mk 9, 28-29). (A variant reading has, "by prayer and fasting").

Christ points out the nexus between prayer and the power that a person has over the forces of evil. The first implication is obvious. Jesus himself had this power which came from prayer, while apparently the disciples did not have it. It is a power they will receive when they receive the gift of the Spirit on Pentecost. Christ is filled with the Spirit. The power of his prayer is the power of the Spirit within him, a power which knows no bounds. Later, as Christ prophesied, "In my name they will cast out devils" (Mk 16, 17). This will take place through the gift of the Spirit.

In another passage in Mark we find that the efficacy of prayer depends on the strength of our faith and also on the disposition of our love for others. "I tell you solemnly, if anyone says to this mountain, 'Get up and throw yourself into the sea,' with no hesitation in his heart but believing that what he says will happen, it will be done for him. I tell you therefore: everything you ask and pray for, believe that you have it already, and it will be yours. And when you stand in prayer, forgive whatever you have against anybody, so that your Father in heaven may forgive your failings too" (Mk 11, 23–25).

This is not the place to give a treatise on the nature of faith as we find it in the gospels. But if the vitality of our prayer depends on the vitality of our faith, we have to understand to some extent the nature of faith. Faith, first of all, has nothing to do with magic. We might jump to the conclusion from the example that Jesus uses about faith moving the mountain that faith has a certain magic quality about it. When it is there, the effect takes place automatically. This would put faith on the level of physical energy or force. If such a force is there, the effect will follow, and the effect is measured by the force which is applied. This type of thinking has no appreciation of the meaning of faith.

Throughout the gospels Jesus is described as seeking this faith, arousing it, increasing it. We never read that he was filled with amazement at any human achievement. But he was filled with amazement at the achievement of faith. On the occasion when the centurion asked that Jesus cure his servant, and expressed his faith in the power of Jesus, we read, "When Jesus heard this he was astonished and said to those following him, 'I tell you solemnly, nowhere in Israel have I found faith like this' " (Mt 8, 10).

Faith can be described as the basic willingness to be led by God, not as God is known through reason, but through his entrance into history. Faith is the response to an invitation, a calling, a vocation, which is known only through God's action in history. It is a disposition which affects the whole man, what he believes, what he thinks, and what he does. He not only gives his understanding over to God's revelation to be led to the truth; he gives his will, his affections, his whole being over to God to be led by him, as he has revealed himself.

Faith, then, is always related to history. It is rooted in what God has done in the past, in his saving acts as well as in his saving words. These saving acts in the past serve as an anchor for faith. But they also point to the future. They indicate whither God wishes to lead, if one opens himself to God's calling.

Our faith opens us not to the God of the world or the God of nature, but to the God of history (who, of course, is also the God of nature). The strength of our faith is measured by the degree to which one allows the God of history to direct one's life. Practically speaking it means the degree to which one allows Christ to direct one's life, not in some abstract way, but in and through the church. Only in this way does the word of the Lord of history, which is past, become the word of the Lord of history who is present.

Faith can be described (as is traditional) as an assent. But it is an assent to what God is, through assenting to what God has done, as well as what God intends to do.

It is, of course, at the same time assent to the declarations which define what God is and what he has done. Otherwise our assent becomes meaningless. One cannot assent to another's overtures unless one knows the meaning of the overtures. In assenting to God's leading-love, it is necessary to assent to the meaning which that leading-love has. This is declared through the teaching of the church.

As the Lord of history, God's activity in time creates a pattern or a design, which has stages of fulfilment. The whole of the pattern is called the divine economy. This divine economy is initiated by God, but it is formed also of man's response. It is not only God acting in us, as if we were robots. The divine economy is a pattern made of a twofold gift, two acts of freedom, that of God, and that of man. But to meet God's act of freedom man must stand out and free himself from the limitations which surround him. This ecstasy (which literally means a "standing out") is what is meant by faith. A person must stand out in order to allow himself to be led by God. This is not possible through human endeavor alone. It must come about through God's creative power, which draws a person out of what is merely natural, so that he can live in this ecstasy of faith.

To return to the comparison which Christ uses—if a man's faith is strong enough he can even move mountains. The comparison is meant to show the power of faith, because from a man's experience he knows it would take great power to move a mountain. The power of faith is such that it can re-order the whole world of things and draw them into the new order of God's kingdom. The re-ordering of things takes place in an ordinary way in the daily life of the Christian; it can also take place in an extraordinary way, in a miracle, which acts as a sign of the re-ordering of all things which is taking place in an invisible way. A miracle is, as it were, a coming to the surface of the re-ordering which is taking place at the heart of reality. But the most important re-ordering that takes place through faith is a re-ordering in the heart of man. This is the mountain which is moved through faith. All other signs which are related to faith are subordinate to, and directed to, changing man's heart. Wind and rain can eventually move a mountain. But no amount of physical force can move, can re-order a man's heart. This is the miracle of faith.

There is a close and necessary connection between the signs which Christ performed, the faith of the bystanders, and the re-ordering of the human heart. We read that Christ did not perform many miracles in his own hometown of Nazareth. "He did not work many miracles there because of their lack of faith" (Mt 13, 58). It is not that he lacked the power to perform the signs, but signs performed before blind people are useless. Their blindness was not physical but a blindness of the heart. The signs are performed before those who see, or at least want to see, and they are intended to open a person's sight even more, by opening his heart.

Perhaps we seem to have strayed from our main point, the relationship of prayer and faith. But prayer is faith speaking. It is giving words to that which we believe. Prayer shares in our weakness, since it speaks of our needs, but it shares in God's strength, because it has the force of faith behind it. In this way prayer is more

forceful than any physical force, because it has behind it
the power of God. We might be praying always to move
mountains, and see no visible effect. The mountain is
still there. But the prayer is re-ordering our own heart
and the hearts of others. Every prayer is answered with
the gift of the Spirit. This gift may be less appreciated
than the other objects we pray for, which also can be
granted in God's loving providence. But it is the gift to
which all other things are ordered. We could recall the
words of St. Paul, "Be ambitious for the higher gifts.
And I am going to show you a way that is better than
any of them" (I Co 12, 31). And he proceeds to describe the gift of love.

This brings us back to the passage which initiated our
discussion of faith. Our prayer is not only the expression of the power of our faith; it is also the expression
of our love. "And when you stand in prayer, forgive
whatever you have against anybody, so that your Father
in heaven may forgive your failings too" (Mk 11,25). In
our prayer we not only stand in the presence of the
Father; we also stand in the presence of our brethren.
We cannot close our hearts to our brethren and open
them to the Father. Such prayer would be insincere.

In chapter eighteen of Luke we find other qualities of
prayer mentioned. It should be constant and it should
be humble. "He spoke to them in a parable to show that
they should keep on praying and never lose heart.
"There was once a judge who cared nothing for God or
man, and in the same town there was a widow who
constantly came before him demanding justice against
her opponent. For a long time he refused; but in the end
he said to himself, "True, I care nothing for God or

man; but this widow is so great a nuisance that I will see her righted before she wears me out with her persistence." ' The Lord said, 'You hear what the unjust judge says; and will not God vindicate his chosen, who cry out to him day and night while he listens patiently to them? I tell you, he will vindicate them soon enough. But when the Son of Man comes, will he find faith on earth?' " (Lk 18,1–8).

The passage seems to be directed to the Christian community who are under stress of persecution. It is a grave injustice that those who bring the good news of salvation should be treated this way, just as the widow, who has no husband to help her, is being treated unfairly both by her opponent and by the judge.

The lesson is this. The judge finally metes out justice to her not because of the rightness or wrongness of her case, but because she would not leave him alone. If this is true with a judge who does not even care for the rightness or wrongness of the issue, will not the heavenly Father, who is just, vindicate his chosen ones who have right on their side. Even when the Son of Man comes again, he will not find the situation reversed. He will still find his community of faithful praying for justice, while they are being oppressed by those who reject the gospel.

This prayer for vindication reminds us of a prayer from the Apocalypse. "When he broke the fifth seal, I saw underneath the altar the souls of those who had been slaughtered for God's word and for the testimony they bore. They gave a great cry, 'How long, sovereign Lord, holy and true, must it be before thou wilt vindicate us and avenge our blood on the inhabitants of the earth?' Each of them was given a white robe; and they were told to rest a little while longer, until the tally should be complete of all their brothers in Christ's service who were to be killed as they had been" (Rv 6, 9–10). This is not a prayer for vengeance but a prayer that the theophany which is God's kingdom become manifest. The manifestation of his kingdom is a day of salvation and also a day of judgment. On this day his chosen ones will be vindicated.

There is another parable which follows. It brings out the need for humility in our prayer. This time Luke helps us out by telling us the purpose of the parable. "It was aimed at those who were sure of their own goodness and looked down on everyone else. 'Two men went up to the temple to pray, one a Pharisee and the other a tax-gatherer. The Pharisee stood up and prayed thus: "I thank thee, O God, that I am not like the rest of men, greedy, dishonest, adulterous; or for that matter, like this tax-gatherer. I fast twice a week; I pay tithes on all that I get." But the other kept his distance and would not even raise his eyes to heaven, but beat upon his breast, saying, "O God, have mercy on me, sinner that I am." It was this man, I tell you, and not the other, who went home acquitted of his sins. For everyone who exalts himself will be humbled; and whoever humbles himself will be exalted' " (Lk 18,9–14).

The prayer of the Pharisee is not a prayer in which his needs are exposed to God, but rather one in which his self-sufficiency is displayed. Though he says that he is thanking God, his thanks are not given for the gifts which he has received, but for the differences which he finds between himself and others. His attitude was accompanied by the scorn that usually belongs to the one who, as Luke says, is sure of his own goodness. It is instructive for us to compare this so-called prayer with the *Magnificat* of Mary. She recounts the gifts which God has given to her, always conscious of the fact that God had looked on the lowliness of his handmaid and had raised her up, so that all nations would call her blessed.

The external performance of prayer without the right interior disposition is condemned again by Jesus in another passage. "Beware of lawyers who love to walk up and down in long robes, and have a great liking for respectful greetings in the street. These are the men who eat up the property of widows, while they say long prayers for appearances' sake; they will receive the severest sentence" (Lk 20,45–47). This is a very severe condemnation. But it is deserved. There is real perversion where the external words and actions are in contradiction to the attitude of the heart. It is a lie, but a special kind of lie. It is a hypocrisy in what is most sacred, our relationship to God. Prayer has simply become a device to get something from men rather than an expression of our relationship to God.

Our Lord describes the necessity of prayer during the dangers which will accompany the last days. "Be on the alert, praying at all times for strength to pass safely through all these imminent troubles and to stand in the presence of the Son of Man" (Lk 21,36). Our strength will come from our constant prayer. In this way we shall be able to stand unashamedly in the presence of Jesus when he comes. This same notion is brought out when

Jesus tells his disciples at the time of his agony, " 'Pray that you may be spared the hour of testing' . . . . When he rose from prayer and came to the disciples he found them asleep, worn out by grief. 'Why are you sleeping?' he said. 'Rise and pray that you may be spared the test' " (Lk 22, 40, 45-46).

It is through prayer that we acquire the strength to pass through the test, whatever that test might be in God's providence. To be tested means to find out what we really are. This means that a situation in life acts as a kind of proof to bring out what we are. Like the chemicals which bring out the images on the photograph our life situations manifest what we are. But what we are depends fundamentally on what we want or on what we love. That is why these situations manifest what we really want or what we really love. This is where prayer plays its chief role. It is only through prayer that we begin to re-order our lives. We begin to know what we really need and to want what we really need. Prayer strengthens our power to love, and to adhere to what we love, no matter what the difficulties are. In this way prayer helps us withstand the test.

The final verse of Luke's gospel describes how the disciples returned to Jerusalem after the ascension and "spent all their time in the temple praising God" (Lk 24,52–53).

We would like to summarize the results of our reflections on the nature of Christian prayer as we find it in the synoptic gospels, especially the Gospel of Luke.

The first thing which strikes us is the important place given to instruction about prayer. Not in the whole of the Old Testament do we find as much instruction on how to pray, the characteristics of prayer, the distinctions between true prayer and what is mere formalism. Though the Old Testament, especially the psalms, brings out the place of prayer in the life of Israel, we do not find there a pedagogy of prayer. In the synoptics, on the other hand, Jesus is constantly teaching the Christians how to pray. Though the disciples asked him only once to teach them how to pray, his instruction was not limited to giving them the Lord's Prayer. It is distributed throughout the whole of the gospel. The fact that this instruction was preserved for us by the evangelists shows how important they felt this was. It also undoubtedly reflects the prayer life of the Christian community at the time when the gospels were written. But behind the evangelists' purpose and behind the life of the community lay the realization that their new mode of existence as Christians meant a new relationship to the Father. This new life had to express itself in prayer.

As we find Christian prayer in the synoptics, it means prayer to the Father that his will be done, and prayer for what the children of the Father need. What the Father wills is the coming of his kingdom. Therefore prayer is always concerned with this explicitly or implicitly. The needs of the children are manifold—the need for their daily bread, which takes in all of their physical and social needs; the need for forgiveness; the need for strength in the hour of trial; and the need for perseverance as children of the Father.

THE PRAYER OF THE CHRISTIAN IN THE SYNOPTICS

The characteristics of Christian prayer are the following: it proceeds from a lively faith; it shows a deep confidence in God our heavenly Father; it is constant, and finally it is humble.

2. The Prayer Of The Christian In The Gospel Of St. John

All of the material which is directly concerned with prayer in the Fourth Gospel is found in the discourse at the Last Supper. The whole gospel is concerned with the Christian's new orientation to the Father. His whole life is one of worship "in spirit and truth," that is, worship which belongs to the final age, the age of the Spirit. But the remarks of Jesus which are directly concerned with prayer occur within the context of the Last Supper.

We shall notice a development here over what we have seen in the synoptics. There the stress was on the prayer which we offer to the Father as his children. Here the explicit note of Christ's mediatorship is brought out. Further the role of the Holy Spirit, which is not brought out explicitly in the synoptics, is brought to the fore in the Gospel of John.

The prayer described there is mainly the prayer of petition. "Indeed, anything you ask in my name I will do, so that the Father may be glorified in the Son. If you ask anything in my name I will do it. If you love me you will obey my commands; and I will ask the Father, and he will give you another to be your Advocate, who

99

will be with you forever—the Spirit of Truth" (Jn 14, 13-16). "I appoint you to go on and bear fruit, fruit that shall last; so that the Father may give you all that you ask in my name" (Jn 15, 16). "I shall see you again, and then you will be joyful, and no one shall rob you of your joy. When that day comes you will ask nothing of me. In very truth I tell you, if you ask the Father for anything in my name, he will give it to you. So far you have asked nothing in my name. Ask and you will receive, that your joy may be complete" (Jn 16, 23-26). "When that day comes you will make your request in my name, and I do not say that I shall pray to the Father for you, for the Father loves you himself, because you have loved me and believed that I came forth from God" (Jn 16, 26-27).

These are the texts in John which deal with prayer. The ideas here are not put forth in a systematic way. There are currents of thought which occur and re-occur, and which cross one another. In crossing one another they even seem to contradict one another. This does not mean that there is no development or progress in the thought. But the development takes place through the constant interweaving of various themes until the final pattern emerges.

The basic idea which underlies all that John says about prayer is that the Christians have a new power to pray when Jesus returns to the Father. The Trinitarian nature of our prayer is revealed. We can direct our prayers to the Father in the name of Jesus. We can also direct our prayers to Jesus himself. Both the Father and Jesus himself will listen to our prayer and grant our request. The fact that Jesus is going away does not mean that they are losing their advocate. On the contrary he will give them another Advocate who will be with them forever.

It is striking that prayer is described here only in terms of asking, that is, the prayer of petition. Perhaps the word "asking" does not have a very rich connotation for us. It has a richer connotation for John than it does for us. The notion of asking is intimately related to the realization of what God wants to give. Only if we have a realization of what God wants to give can we ask as we should. Jesus said to the Samaritan woman, "If only you knew what God gives, and who it is that is asking you for a drink, you would have asked him and he would have given you living water" (Jn 4, 10). The whole Christian attitude is a matter of growing to realize what God wants to give and then to ask for it. It is expressed in the prayer of the woman when she said, "Sir, give me that water, and then I shall not be thirsty, nor have to come all this way to draw" (Jn 4, 15).

The power to know the gift and to ask for it will come with the gift of the Spirit. But the Spirit will be given only when Jesus is glorified. "On the last and greatest day of the festival Jesus stood and cried aloud, 'If anyone is thirsty let him come to me; whoever believes in me, let him drink.' As Scripture says, 'Streams of living water shall flow out from within him.' He was speaking of the Spirit which believers in him would receive later; for the Spirit had not yet been given, because Jesus had not yet been glorified" (Jn 7, 37-39). When the Spirit is given, the whole gift of Christ is given. But with the gift there is also a new power to ask. Our prayer also receives a new direction, not simply from the outside, but from the life which is within the

Christian. The Christian can pray to the Father through Jesus, or in the name of Jesus, and he can pray also to Jesus. Both he and the Father will grant the request. The Father answers the requests as Father, as the origin of all good things. The Son answers as the mediator of these gifts to men.

We see, then, that John does not have a great deal to say about prayer when we look only at the number of passages which are concerned with prayer. But what he says is a significant development over the synoptics. Christian prayer becomes situated and defined not only by its relationship to the Father, but through the relationship it has to Jesus as *advocate with the Father*, and through the relationship it has to the Spirit as *advocate with us*. Christian prayer begins to take on the characteristics which the prayer of Christ has in the Gospel of John. It is prayer from within a union, or within communion. While the communion is already realized, it is also seeking for fulfilment, for completeness. Our prayer is our way of asking for that completeness.

When we read these passages in John which have to do with prayer, we sometimes feel that there is a "credibility gap" between the promises and the actual fact. Christ uses words which are comprehensive in their meaning, "*anything* you ask . . . the Father will give you *all* that you ask." The asking which Jesus is speaking about is that asking which belongs to the era of the Spirit. It is asking which could be described as eschatological. This means that it has the marks of the endtime, the time marked by God's definitive gift of his Word and his Spirit. It has as its source the gift of the Spirit, and its object are those gifts which formed the object of Jesus' own prayer (cf. Jn 17). Sometimes our prayer is like that of the mother of Zebedee's sons who came with her sons to make a request of Jesus. She asked for special places for her sons in the kingdom. Jesus told her, "You do not know what you are asking" (Mt 20, 22). When we do not know what we are asking, Jesus tries to change what we are asking for, in order that our request further the kingdom of God. Often this comes through a new and deeper meaning of our part in the kingdom of God. This was the approach which Jesus used with the sons of Zebedee. He asked them, 'Can you drink the cup that I am going to drink?' They replied, We can.' 'Very well,' he said you shall drink my cup, but as for seats at my right hand and my left, these are not mine to grant; they belong to those to whom they have been allotted by my Father' " (Mt 20, 22-23). He tried to change their prayer by bringing home to them the role they would play in the kingdom through sharing in his passion.

When we realize the eschatological nature of our prayer, the words Jesus uses to describe how completely our prayer will be answered are not exaggerations proper to oriental ways of expression. They are literally true. We learn more and more what to ask for as we realize the nature of Christ's kingdom and our role in it. In this way all of our prayer in one way or another is the prayer, "Thy kingdom come."

3. The Prayer Of The Christian In The Acts of The Apostles

In *Acts* there is no explicit instruction concerning Christian prayer. As the name of the book indicates, it is concerned with the record of the activities of the early Christian community. But, even though there are no specific instructions on prayer, we see that prayer is one of the activities of the community.

The way we first meet the Christian community in *Acts* is as a community assembled in prayer. "All these were constantly at prayer together, and with them a group of women, including Mary the mother of Jesus and his brothers" (Ac 1, 14). In choosing the one who was to take the place of Judas they prayed. "Then they prayed and said, 'Thou, Lord who knowest the hearts of all men, declare which of these two thou hast chosen to receive this office of ministry and apostleship." (Ac 1, 24). After Pentecost they lived their lives in an atmosphere of prayer. "With one mind they kept up their daily attendance at the temple, and, breaking bread in private houses, shared their meals with unaffected joy, as they praised God and enjoyed the favor of the whole people" (Ac 2, 46-47). The first miracle performed by

Peter took place as he was on his way to the temple to pray. "One day at three in the afternoon, the hour of prayer, Peter and John were on their way up to the temple." (Ac 3, 1). The description of the cure of the cripple follows. When Peter and John were released from prison, they returned to their brethern. The spontaneous reaction was one of prayer. "They raised their voices as one man and called upon God: 'Sovereign Lord, maker of heaven and earth and sea and of everything in them, who by the Holy Spirit, through the mouth of David, thy servant, didst say, "Why did the Gentiles rage and peoples lay their plots in vain? The kings of the earth took their stand and the rulers made common cause against the Lord and against his Messiah." They did indeed make common cause in this very city against they holy servant Jesus whom thou didst anoint as Messiah. Herod and Pontius Pilate conspired with the Gentiles and peoples of Israel to do all the things which, under thy hand and by thy decree, were foreordained. And now, O Lord, mark their threats, and enable thy servants to speak thy word with all boldness. Stretch out thy hand to heal and cause signs and wonders to be done through the name of thy holy servant Jesus.' When they had ended their prayer, the building where they were assembled rocked, and all were filled with the Holy Spirit and spoke the word of God with boldness" (Ac 4, 24-31).

This prayer is noteworthy for many reasons. It follows the Old Testament models of prayer. These prayers usually come after a manifestation of God's saving power. The prayer is made up of an invocation of God, then a recalling of God's saving acts and his promises, and finally a petition. When the prayer was concluded there was a sign of the presence of God. The building rocked. Such signs like the storm, the wind, the earthquake, are common Old Testament signs of the presence of God.

This prayer is like the sermons in the early part of *Acts.* It is still Old Testament in its tone. They realized with praise and gratitude that God had fulfilled his promises to the people of Israel through sending Jesus his Messiah.

We find, however, in the prayer of Stephen the awareness which carries with it the seeds of later development concerning the place of Christ as mediator. In the account of the martyrdom of Stephen we see one of the earliest prayers made directly to Christ. "But Stephen, filled with the Holy Spirit, and gazing intently up to heaven, saw the glory of God, and Jesus standing at God's right hand. 'Look,' he said, 'there is a rift in the sky; I can see the Son of Man standing at God's right hand.'. . . So they stoned Stephen, and as they did so, he called out, 'Lord Jesus, receive my spirit.' Then he fell on his knees and cried aloud, 'Lord, do not hold this sin against them,' and with that he died" (Ac 7, 55-60). In this prayer the old merges with the new. The title "Son of Man" which Jesus used of himself is used here by Stephen, but it will fade into disuse, giving way to the title "Lord" which Stephen also uses. As Christ committed his spirit to the Father when he died, so now Stephen commits his spirit to Christ. His own prayer is an echo of Christ's prayer when he prayed for those executing him, that they might be forgiven. In committing his spirit to Christ he is expressing that basic awareness that alive or dead he belongs to the Lord. As St. Paul, who looked on the murder with approval, would later write, "For no one of us lives, and equally no one of us dies, for himself alone. If we live, we live for the Lord; and if we die, we die for the Lord. Whether therefore we live or die, we belong to the Lord" (Rm 14, 7-8). With his dying breath Stephen proclaimed that he belonged to the Lord.

One of the reasons given for the appointment of seven deacons to help with the work of the apostles was to enable the apostles more time to devote themselves to prayer and to the ministry of the Word (Ac 6, 4). The deacons were ordained with prayer and imposition of hands (Ac 6, 6). When Peter and John went to Samaria, after they had heard that Samaria had accepted the word of God, they prayed for the converts, asking that they might receive the Holy Spirit. Then they imposed their hands on them and they received the Holy Spirit (Ac 8, 15-17).

When we first come upon Saul after his conversion we find him at prayer. The Lord told Ananias, "Go at once to Straight Street, to the house of Judas, and ask for a man from Tarsus named Saul. You will find him at prayer" (Ac 9, 11-12). When Peter performed the miracle of raising Dorcas, it is mentioned that "he knelt down and prayed" (Ac 9, 40). Cornelius who was the first of the Gentiles to receive the faith is described as a man who "was regular in his prayers to God" (Ac 10, 2). Peter himself was at prayer when the messengers came from Cornelius. Cornelius affirms that it was while he was at prayer that he had the vision commanding him to send for Peter. "Four days ago, just about this time, I was in the house here saying the afternoon prayers, when suddenly a man in shining robes stood before me"

(Ac 10, 30). This is a very important incident in the *Acts*—the reception of the first Gentile convert. The communication of God's will to Cornelius and to Peter took place at the time of their prayer.

When Peter was released from prison through miraculous intervention, 'he went to the house of Mary, the mother of John Mark, where a large company was at prayer" (Ac 12, 12). The mission of Paul and Barnabas to the Gentiles was settled upon after prayer. "While they were keeping a fast and offering worship to the Lord, the Holy Spirit said, 'set Barnabas and Saul apart for me, to do the work to which I have called them.' Then, after further fasting and prayer, they laid their hands on them and let them go" (Ac 13, 2-3). On their missionary journey they appointed presbyters for the churches after prayer and fasting: "They also appointed elders for them in each congregation, and with prayer and fasting committed them to the Lord in whom they had put their faith" (Ac 14, 23).

When Paul and his companions came to Philippi, they were on their way to the place of prayer, when they met the slave-girl who was possessed by a divining spirit. When Paul drove this spirit out, the mob was aroused. They were seized, beaten, thrown into prison. While in prison they prayed. "About midnight Paul and Silas, at their prayers, werê singing praises to God, and the other prisoners were listening" (Ac 16, 25-26). The account of their deliverance from prison follows.

Paul received his strength and encouragement from Christ in his prayer. "One night in a vision the Lord said to Paul, 'Have no fear: go on with your preaching and do not be silenced, for I am with you and no one shall attempt to do you harm; and there are many in this city who are my people' " (Ac 18, 9-10).

When Paul said his farewell to the elders whom he had summoned from Ephesus, they prayed together. Their prayer is described in a very touching way. "As he finished speaking he knelt down with them all and prayed. Then there were loud cries of sorrow from them all, as they folded Paul in their arms and kissed him" (Ac 20, 36-37). Paul prayed when he exercised the charismatic power of curing the sick. He cured the father of the magistrate on the island of Malta. "Paul visited him and, after prayer, laid his hands upon him and healed him; whereupon the other sick people on the island came also and were cured" (Ac 28, 8-9).

When Paul finally arrived at Rome, and was met there by the Christians, his first act was one of prayerful thanks. "The Christians there had news of us and came out to meet us as far as Appii Forum and Tres Tabernae, and when Paul saw them, he gave thanks to God and took courage" (Ac 28, 15).

As was mentioned when we began our consideration of prayer in *Acts,* there is little there in terms of formal instruction about prayer. But we see that for the Christians and the Christian community prayer was part of their normal life. We would have a very different idea of the early Christians if we omitted the passages concerning prayer from *Acts.* We find the community at prayer, and we find individuals praying — Peter, John, Stephen, Saul, Cornelius. We find prayer of every kind and in every situation — prayer for enlightment and direction, prayer of petition, of praise, of thanks, prayer for forgiveness of enemies, prayer for the converts, prayer for the missionary journeys. Prayer goes with them wherever they go, whether in the community in the breaking of the bread, or in prison, or on the rooftop, or on the seashore, or in the synagogue.

The *Acts* is concerned with the movement of the Christian message from Jerusalem into the pagan world. This movement is always accompanied by prayer.

4. The Prayer Of The Christian In The Apocalypse

The *Apocalypse* (or *The Book of Revelation*) is probably the most prayerful book of the New Testament. It is filled with the atmosphere of adoration and praise. In the other books of the New Testament we find a great deal concerning the prayer of petition. In the *Apocalypse* we find a broader description of prayer; the prayer of the Christian and his worship are drawn into a closer unity. Christ is not only the one who is our intercessor, and the one to whom we can pray. He can receive our adoration, the same adoration which is given to the Father.

The *Apocalypse* is, then, particularly instructive in showing us the liturgical prayer of the Christian. This does not mean to say that the prayers in the *Apocalypse* were part of the early Christian liturgy. Rather they show the whole spirit behind Christian liturgy, that of worship and of praise given to the Father and to the Son through the gift of his Spirit. The language is for the most part that of the Old Testament. But the meaning is entirely different. As all things "are made new" (Rv 21, 5), so also Christian worship. It is made new through the redemption.

The Christ who is described there as the object of our worship is the same Christ as the Christ of the gospels. But now he has taken on the attributes of Lordship, won through his redemptive life. Yet his Lordship does not separate him from the church. On the contrary, he moves in and among the lampstands which symbolize his church.

The *Apocalypse* is a closed book to most Christians because of its strange style and obscure symbolism. This is understandable but unfortunate. It is a book which has much to teach concerning the meaning of Christ and the life of the Christian. One who would take the patience to understand the literary medium the author is using would be amply rewarded.

The setting for the whole of the *Apocalypse* is given in the first chapter. Christ appears clothed as a priest. His attributes are described through symbols. He is present among the lamps, which symbolize the churches. He tells John, "Write down therefore what you have seen, what is now, and what will be hereafter" (Rv 1, 19). The message comes from Christ the priest, present among the faithful. Much of the message will have to do with the worship his priestly people give him and the Father. As John says, "To him who loves us and freed us from our sins with his life's blood, who made of us a royal house, to serve as priests of his God and Father— to him be glory and dominion for ever and ever! Amen" (Rv 1, 5-6). He is a priest and has made his people a priestly people. The doxology which is given to Christ here is typical of prayer in the *Apocalypse*.

Following the description of the vision John had of Christ as high priest there are seven letters addressed to seven of the churches in Asia Minor. Some passages are instructive for us in the matter of prayer.

Significantly in one of his letters, Jesus is called the "Amen" of God. "Here is the message of the Amen, the faithful, the true witness, the ultimate source of God's creation" (Rv 3, 14). This means that Jesus is the answer to all that God has promised. He is God's complete yes. But he is not only God's yes to his promises. He is also the complete fulfilment of our prayers. When we terminate our prayers with the words "through Christ our Lord" we are saying that not only is Jesus our mediator with the Father. He is also the Father's "amen" to all our prayers.

In the last of the letters to the seven churches Christ is portrayed as knocking at the door of men's hearts. "Look, I am standing at the door, knocking. If one of you hears me calling and opens the door, I will come in to share his meal, side by side with him. Those who prove victorious I will allow to share my throne, just as I was victorious myself and took my place with my Father on his throne" (Rv 3, 20-21). In the gospel we were told that if one knocked the door would be opened. Here Christ himself is described as the one who is knocking. This gives us a more complete view of prayer. Our own prayer is really a response to Christ himself, whose activity precedes ours. We also see that every prayer is answered in an eminent way. Prayer always opens the door to closer union with Christ.

There follows one of the most majestic scenes in Scripture. We see in symbolic terms the whole world turned toward God in praise and adoration. The seer beholds a throne in heaven. On the throne a person is sitting. It is hard to capture the feelings created by the symbolic language. The one who is reigning is described only in terms of precious stones: "and the one sitting there looked like a diamond and a ruby" (Rv 4, 3). There is the brilliance of the diamond and the soft depth of the ruby. His life and light reach out into the sea of glass between the throne and the seer. He is present throughout the sea of glass, and at the same time his presence is concentrated in himself. There is intensity of life but without any motion. There is closeness but at the same time distance that comes from the depth of his life.

There are twenty-four elders surrounding the throne. They represent the church of the Old Testament and the New. Before the throne are seven lamps, called the seven spirits of God, that is, the fulness or perfection of spirit. Round about the throne are four living creatures. They represent the whole of creation. They chant a hymn day and night without ceasing. "Holy, holy, holy is God the sovereign Lord of all, who was and is, and is to come!" (Rv 4, 8). At the same time the elders add their worship: "Every time the animals glorified and honored and gave thanks to the One sitting on the throne, who lives forever and ever, the twenty-four elders prostrated themselves before him to worship the One who lives forever and ever, and threw down their crowns in front of the throne, saying, 'You are our Lord and our God, you are worthy of glory and honor and power, because you made all the universe and it was only by your will that everything was made and exists' " (Rv 4, 9-11).

In one harmoniously synchronized act of worship the whole of creation adores the One on the throne. With the external act of adoration shown in the act of prostration and throwing their crowns before the throne, there is the song of honor, praise, and thanks. The One who is on the throne is worthy of this, because he is God, Lord, creator of the world, the holy One, the One who is from everlasting to everlasting.

Immediately after this, the Lamb appears, to take up the scroll of history. "Then I saw, standing between the throne with its four animals and the circle of the elders, a Lamb that seemed to have been sacrificed . . . . The Lamb came forward to take the scroll from the right hand of the One sitting on the throne, and when he took it, the four animals prostrated themselves before him and with them the twenty-four elders; each one of them was holding a harp and had a golden bowl full of incense made of the prayers of the saints" (Rv 5, 6-8). They burst into a new song; it is new because it has to do with the final revelation of God among men through the redemption in his Son. "They sang a new hymn: 'You are worthy to take the scroll and break the seals of it, because you were sacrificed, and with your blood you bought men for God of every race, language, people and nation and made them a line of kings and priests, to serve our God and to rule the world' " (Rv 5, 9-10).

But immediately thousands of other voices are added to those of the elders, praising the Son. His redemptive work has cosmic effects. Even the angels join in the praise. "In my vision, I heard the sound of an immense number of angels gathered round the throne and the animals and the elders; there were ten thousand times ten thousand of them and thousands upon thousands, shouting, 'The Lamb that was sacrificed is worthy to be given power, riches, wisdom, strength, honor, glory and blessing. Then I heard all the living things in creation—everything that lives in the air, and on the ground, and

117

in the sea, crying, 'To the One who is sitting on the throne and to the Lamb, be all praise, honor, glory and power, forever and ever.' And the four animals said 'Amen', and the elders prostrated themselves to worship" (Rv 5, 11-14).

There is no honor in the whole of creation which is not due to the Lamb. There is no voice in the whole of creation which does not lift itself in praise of the Lamb. There is no living thing which does not pay its adoration to the One on the throne and to the Lamb.

In the episodes which follow, the Lamb proceeds to break the seals on the scroll of history. He breaks them one by one. Just before he breaks the seventh and final seal a paean of praise is given to God and to the Lamb by those who have been redeemed. "After that I saw a huge number, impossible to count, of people from every nation, race, tribe and language; they were standing in front of the throne and in front of the Lamb, dressed in white robes and holding palms in their hands. They shouted aloud, 'Victory to our God, who sits on the throne, and to the Lamb!' " (Rv 7, 9-10). The seer is thinking chiefly of the martyrs who have offered their lives to God in imitation of the Lamb. But their victory is really God's victory. They acknowledge the source of their own power to overcome, power from the One on the throne and from the Lamb.

Immediately the rest of creation adds its praise to that of the saints. "And all the angels who were standing in a circle round the throne, surrounding the elders and the four animals, prostrated themselves before the throne, and touched the ground with their foreheads, worshipping God with these words, 'Amen. Praise and glory and wisdom and thanksgiving and honor and pow-

er and strength to our God forever and ever. Amen' "
(Rv 7, 11-12).

Then the seven angels with trumpets announce some
aspect of the coming of the Day of the Lord. But before
they begin to play their part in this symbolic drama,
another angel is seen offering the prayers of the saints to
God. "Then another angel came and stood at the altar,
holding a golden censer; and he was given a great quan-
tity of incense to offer with the prayers of all God's
people upon the golden altar in front of the throne. And
from the angel's hand the smoke of the incense went up
before God with the prayers of his people" (Rv 8, 3-4).
Throughout this drama there is collaboration between
the world of angels and that of the saints. They praise
God and the Lamb together, they offer the prayers of
the saints to God, and they also play a role in overcoming the powers of evil.

When the seventh angel blows his trumpet, it is the
sign that time and history are at an end. The world has
passed into the hands of the one who redeemed it. It is
an occasion for praise and thanksgiving. "Then the
seventh angel blew his trumpet, and voices could be
heard shouting in heaven, calling, 'The kingdom of the
world has become the kingdom of our Lord and his
Christ, and he will reign forever and ever.' The twenty-
four elders, enthroned in the presence of God, prostrated themselves and touched the ground with their
foreheads worshipping God with these words, 'We give
thanks to you, Almighty Lord God, He-Is-and-He-Was,
for using your great power and beginning your reign.
The nations were seething with rage and now the time
has come for your own anger, and for the dead to be
judged, and for your servants the prophets, for the

saints and for all who worship you, small or great, to be rewarded. The time has come to destroy those who are destroying the earth' " (Rv 11, 15-18).

Among the various hymns of praise in the *Apocalypse* one belongs to a particular group. It can be sung only by those who have kept their virginity. Here the word "virginity" is used in its Old Testament sense to describe fidelity to God in overcoming the temptations of idolatry. "Next in my vision I saw Mount Zion, and standing on it a Lamb who had with him a hundred and forty-four thousand people, all with his name, and his Father's name written on their foreheads. I heard a sound coming out of the sky like the sound of the ocean or the roar of thunder; it seemed to be the sound of harpists playing their harps. There in front of the throne they were singing a new hymn in the presence of the four animals and the elders, a hymn that could only be learnt by the hundred and forty-four thousand who had been redeemed from the world. These are the ones who have kept their virginity and not been defiled with women; they follow the Lamb wherever he goes; they have been redeemed from amongst men to be the first-fruits for God and for the Lamb. They never allowed a lie to pass their lips and no fault can be found in them" (Rv 14, 1-5).

In a wider sense this scene describes the prayer of every Christian who is faithful to Christ. Fidelity is described in terms of virginity. Earlier we spoke of the uniqueness of Christian prayer. This uniqueness is described here in a symbolic way, in terms of a song which only they can sing.

Shortly after, these same ones who had remained faithful through persecution sing the song of Moses and the song of the Lamb. They are songs of victory; Moses' victory was a type of Christ's. The seer describes his vision. "I seemed to see a glass lake suffused with fire, and standing by the lake of glass, those who had fought against the beast and won, and against his statue and the number which is his name. They all had harps from God, and they were singing the hymn of Moses, the servant of God, and of the Lamb: 'How great and wonderful are all your works, Lord God Almighty; just and true are all your ways, King of nations. Who would not revere and praise your name, O Lord? You alone are holy, and all the pagans will come and adore you for the many acts of justice you have shown' " (Rv 15, 2-4).

A hymn celebrates the definitive victory of God over the powers of evil, symbolized in the overthrow of Babylon, where these powers are concentrated. It acts as a kind of Hallelujah Chorus in heaven. "After this I seemed to hear the great sound of a huge crowd in heaven, singing, 'Alleluia! Victory and glory and power to our God! . . . ' They sang again, 'Alleluia! The smoke of her will go up forever and ever.' Then the twenty-four elders and the four animals prostrated themselves and worshipped God seated there on his throne, and they cried, 'Amen, Alleluia.' Then a voice came from the throne; it said, 'Praise our God, you servants of his and all who, great or small, revere him.' And I seemed to hear the voices of a huge crowd, like the sound of the ocean or the great roar of thunder, answering, 'Alleluia! The reign of the Lord our God Almighty has begun; let us be glad and joyful and give praise to God, because this is the time for the marriage of the Lamb' " (Rv 19, 2, 3-7).

The last song is one that is sung for the wedding of Christ and his Church. "His bride is ready, and she has been able to dress herself in dazzling white linen, because her linen is made of the good deeds of the saints" (Rv 19, 8).

When the seer describes the heavenly Jerusalem, he sees no temple there. There is no particular place marked off from the rest as a place set aside for worship. "I saw no temple in the city; for its temple was the sovereign Lord God and the Lamb. And the city had no need of sun or moon to shine upon it; for the glory of God gave it light, and its lamp was the Lamb" (Rv 21, 22-23). A remarkable transformation has taken place. God and the Lamb have become the place of worship and of prayer.

The *Apocalypse* concludes with a prayer. "The Spirit and the Bride say, 'Come.' Let everyone who listens answer, 'Come.' Then let all who are thirsty come: all who want it may have the water of life, and have it free" (Rv 22, 17). The Spirit and the Bride of Christ, the church, are praying the same prayer. They have the same desire. The desire is for fulfilment of God's kingdom. Christ answers the prayer. "The one who guarantees these revelations repeats his promise: I shall indeed be with you soon. Amen; come, Lord Jesus" (Rv 22, 20).

From what has been said we can see that the *Apocalypse* can teach us a great deal concerning Christian prayer. We could summarize by pointing out the following characteristics of prayer in the *Apocalypse*.

There is the prayer first of all that is the duty of everything that lives to give adoration to God, to praise and to thank him. This is the prayer described in the vision of the elders and the four living creatures in their adoration of the One who is on the throne. There is the prayer of the Christian. He adores with the same adoration both the One on the throne and the Lamb who shares that throne. Christian prayer is always related to the coming of the kingdom of Christ, either in praise and thanks for what has been done, or petition for that which still remains to be done. The Christian who is faithful can sing a song which no other can sing because of his relationship to Christ and to the kingdom of Christ. Finally, it is the Spirit *and* the Bride who pray as one, because they both have one and the same purpose, the fulness of Christ's reign.

We find a significant development in the *Apocalypse* over the synoptics. In the synoptics it is vague how Christ enters into the worship given to the Father. With the Father, as we see in the *Apocalypse*, he is the object of worship. He deserves this worship because he has redeemed us with his blood and in this way he has become the Lord of history. He deserves, then, the prayers of praise, adoration, thanks, petition, which are addressed also to the Father.

5. The Prayer of the Christian in the Letters of St. Paul

Here more than any other place we feel the limitations of this study of prayer in the New Testament. If we wanted to do justice to the meaning of prayer in St. Paul we would have to study it in its relationship to the other major themes of his letters; for example, how it is related to his doctrine of the Holy Spirit, and his theology of faith, hope and love. Since that is not possible here, we want to restrict ourselves to the texts in which he speaks directly about prayer, and from these to get a better understanding of the meaning of Christian prayer.

We shall take these texts as they occur in the letters according to their chronological order, beginning with the letters to the Thessalonians and ending with the Pastoral letters. These letters cover a period of about seventeen years. It is remarkable that, even though the letters differ in theme and show progress in insight into the meaning of Christ, the importance of prayer appears as a constant in all of them. Sometimes we find a special aspect of Christian prayer developed because of a particular theme which Paul is treating in the letter. The chronology which we will follow is that given in the Jerusalem Bible.

a. The Letters To The Thessalonians (50-51 A.D.)

In these earliest letters of St. Paul we find the same characteristics of prayer which will be found in all of

125

the subsequent letters. There is no unified theme in these first two letters, though there is a preoccupation with a particular problem which seems to have been bothering the Thessalonians. This was the problem of judgment and of Jesus' Second Coming.

The first letter begins with the kind of salutation which characterizes all of the subsequent letters of Paul. It was not merely a literary convention. It is a greeting which speaks out the content of his faith in the form of a prayer for his hearers. "From Paul, Silvanus, and Timothy to the congregation of Thessalonians who belong to God the Father and the Lord Jesus Christ. Grace to you and peace. We always thank God for you all, and mention you in our prayers continually. We call to mind, before our God and Father, how your faith has shown itself in action, your love in labor and your hope of our Lord Jesus Christ in fortitude (1 Th 1, 1-3). This forms the pattern for the greeting in his letters—a petition for grace for his hearers, then an act of thanksgiving for their response to the Gospel.

One of the main objects of his prayer, as he goes on to say, is the opportunity to see them again. But now Timothy has just arrived from Thessalonica, bringing good news of your faith and love. He tells us that you always think kindly of us, and are as anxious to see us as we are to see you. And so in all our difficulties and hardships your faith reassures us about you. It is the breath of life to us that you stand firm in the Lord. What thanks can we return to God for you? What thanks for all the joy you have brought us, making us rejoice before our God while we pray most earnestly night and day to be allowed to see you again and to mend your faith where it falls short? May our God and Father himself and our Lord Jesus, bring us direct to you; and may the Lord make your love mount and overflow toward one another and toward all, as our love does towards you. May he make your hearts firm, so that you may stand before our God and Father holy and faultless when our Lord Jesus comes with all those who are his own" (1 Th 3, 6-13). hearts firm, so that you may stand before our God and Father holy and faultless when our Lord Jesus comes with all those who are his own" (1 Th 3, 6-13).

What gives Paul his greatest consolation is the union they have with Christ, a union of faith and of love. His petition is always the same—that they grow in this union and become holy.

The Thessalonians formed a tiny island of Christianity in a sea of paganism. They had many difficulties. Yet he exhorts them to be joyful, and he adds the exhortation to pray. "Be always joyful; pray continually; give thanks whatever happens; for this is what God in Christ wills for you" (1 Th 5, 16-18). He reiterates his petition for them at the close of his letter and asks for their prayers. "May God himself, the God of peace, make you holy in every part, and keep you sound in spirit, soul, and body, without fault when our Lord Jesus Christ comes. He who calls you is to be trusted; he will do it. Brothers, pray for us . . . . The grace of our Lord Jesus Christ be with you" (1 Th 5, 23-28).

In this first letter we find the same ideas which enter into the other letters over the next seventeen years. First of all Paul himself is constantly praying, and he encourages the Christians to pray. Their prayer should be directed to the Father through Jesus Christ. They should give thanks for the graces which they have already received, and beg for those graces they need for even deeper union with Christ. They should also pray for Paul in his apostolate. The result will be to increase the joy which they already have because of their fellowship with one another and Christ. This is the simple but profound theology of prayer of St. Paul.

The second letter to the Thessalonians was written only a few months after the first; the same ideas on prayer characterize both.

In his greeting to them he first recalls their basic relationship to God the Father and to Christ, offers them a greeting in the name of the Father and of Christ, and then offers thanks to God for what he has done for them. "From Paul, Silvanus, and Timothy to the congregation of Thessalonians who belong to God our Father and the Lord Jesus Christ. Our thanks are always due to God for you, brothers. It is right that we should thank him, because your faith increases mightily, and the love you have, each for all and all for each, grows ever greater" (2 Th 1, 2-3). He goes on to describe how proud he is that their faith has remained steadfast under so many persecutions and troubles.

Then he describes the motive and object of his constant prayer for them. "With this in mind we pray for you always, that our God may count you worthy of his calling, and mightily bring to fulfilment every good purpose and every act inspired by faith, so that the name of our Lord Jesus may be glorified in you, and you in him, according to the grace of our God and Lord Jesus Christ" (2 Th 1, 11-12). His prayer, then, is for their fulfilment: that what has begun through God's grace will be brought to fruition so that Christ may be glorified in them.

He then reminds them not to pay attention to those who tell them that the Day of the Lord is near. They should not be upset because they have been chosen by God from the very beginning of time. The fact that God has chosen them is the motive for Paul's thanks. "But we are bound to thank God for you, brothers beloved by the Lord, because from the beginning of time God chose you to find salvation in the Spirit that consecrates you, and in the truth that you believe. It was for this that he called you through the gospel we brought, so that you might possess for your own the splendor of our Lord Jesus Christ" (1 Th 2, 13-14).

Since they are joined in a common brotherhood for a common purpose, he in turn asks for their prayers. He concludes with a prayer for them. "And now, brothers, pray for us, that the word of the Lord may have everywhere the swift and glorious course that it has had among you, and that we may be rescued from wrongheaded and wicked men; for it is not all who have faith" (2 Th 3, 1-2). "May the Lord of peace himself give you peace at all times and in all ways. The Lord be with you all . . . . The grace of our Lord Jesus Christ be with you all (2 Th 3, 16-18).

In the gift of peace are comprised all of the other gifts of grace. He never prays for grace for them except insofar as he prays for peace for them, the peace described in the promises made by God through the prophets and given to us in Christ.

b. The Letters To The Corinthians (57 A.D.)

We do not find a great deal about prayer in the first letter to the Corinthians. His main purpose was to restore unity by getting rid of the factions which had formed. He also wanted to answer some practical questions concerning moral conduct, marriage and virginity, eating of foods consecrated to idols, the regulation of the worship of the community especially in regard to proper discipline in the use of the charismatic gifts. Among the other abuses he wanted to correct was their unchristian behavior when they came together for the celebration of the Eucharist.

There is the usual type of greeting with the prayer for grace and peace. Thanksgiving for the gifts which God has given to them follows. "Grace and peace to you from God our Father and the Lord Jesus Christ. I am always thanking God for you. I thank him for his grace given to you in Christ Jesus" (1 Co 1, 3-4). It is interesting that he emphasizes God's gift to them rather than their response, as he does in other letters. It shows that their vocation has its origin in God's grace. It might also indicate that Paul wanted to point out that their response was not what it should be because of their pride. Their inordinate self-satisfaction is brought out in many places throughout the letter. "There are certain persons who are filled with self-importance because they think I am not coming to Corinth" (4, 18); "your self-satisfaction ill becomes you" (5, 6); "of course we all 'have knowledge', as you say. This 'knowledge' breeds conceit; it is love that builds. If anyone fancies that he knows, he knows nothing yet, in the true sense of knowing. But if a man loves, he is acknowledged by God" (8, 1-3).

He shows them, then, that everything they have is from God, who has been extremely generous to them. "I thank him for all the enrichment that has come to you in Christ. You possess full knowledge and you can give full expression to it, because in you the evidence for the truth of Christ has found confirmation. There is indeed no single gift you lack, while you wait expectantly for our Lord Jesus Christ to reveal himself. He will keep you firm to the end, without reproach on the Day of our Lord Jesus. It is God himself who called you to share in the life of his Son Jesus Christ our Lord; and God keeps faith" (1 Co 1, 5-9).

When Paul speaks about virginity, he is certainly including greater freedom for prayer, though he does not mention this explicitly. "The unmarried or celibate woman cares for the Lord's business; her aim is to be dedicated to him in body as in spirit" (1 Co 7, 3-4). Certainly this care for the Lord's business and total dedication would have one of its expressions in a greater freedom for prayer.

When Paul gives instructions to married couples on the use of their married rights, he advises them in a way which sounds foreign to our secular mentality. It does, however, show the importance he placed on prayer for a married couple. "Do not deny yourselves to one another, except when you agree upon a temporary abstinence in order *to devote yourselves to prayer*" (1 Co 7, 5).

In all of his letters he emphasizes the role that the Holy Spirit plays in Christian prayer. In Galatians, it is the Spirit who enables the Christian to pray. In Romans, the Spirit is said to give us the power to say, "Abba, Father" (Rm 8, 15). Here the Spirit gives us the power to invoke the name of the Lord and to express our faith in him. "No one can say 'Jesus is Lord' except under the influence of the Holy Spirit" (1 Co 12, 3).

The other remarks concerning prayer refer principally to church discipline. He severely reprimands them for their conduct at the eucharistic assembly, which certainly had its effects on the prayer of the assembly. He advises them that along with the gift of ecstatic utterance they should pray for the ability to interpret. "I say, then, that the man who falls into ecstatic utterance should pray for the ability to interpret. If I use such language in my prayer, the Spirit in me prays, but my intellect lies fallow. What then? I will pray as I am inspired to pray, but I will also pray intelligently. I will sing hymns as I am inspired to sing, but I will sing intelligently too. Suppose you are praising God in the language of inspiration: how will the plain man who is present be able to say 'Amen' to your thanksgiving, when he does not know what you are saying? Your prayer of thanksgiving may be all that could be desired, but it is no help to the other man. Thank God, I am more gifted in ecstatic utterance than any of you, but in the congregation I would rather speak five intelligible words for the benefit of others as well as myself, than thousands of words in the language of ecstasy" (1 Co 14, 13-19). The over-all norm to discern the presence of the Spirit in such activity is to see whether it builds up the Church. Though ecstatic utterance may mean something to the one who has the gift, it means nothing to anyone else unless there is someone with the gift of interpretation. It does nothing to build up the church. Paul's emphasis on the fact that our prayer should be intelligible when it is within the congregation is striking. Though he is contrasting intelligible prayer with the unintelligible language of ecstatic utterance, what he says has application to all prayer said in the congregation. Such prayer should speak to the congregation while at the same time it speaks to God.

He concludes his remarks concerning the regulation of their worship by laying down a principle which should guide them. "To sum up, my friends: when you meet for worship, each of you contributes a hymn, some instruction, a revelation, an ecstatic utterance, or the interpretation of such an utterance. All of these must aim at one thing: to build up the church" (1 Co 14, 26-27).

The letter ends with a prayer to Christ, and a prayer for the peace of Christ: "*Marana tha*—Come, O Lord! The grace of the Lord Jesus Christ be with you. My love to you all in Christ Jesus. Amen" (1 Co 16, 22-24).

In conclusion, in First Corinthians there is little explicit teaching on prayer. Paul is occupied with the problems dividing the community, moral and doctrinal problems. Perhaps he gives us a clue why there is so little there on prayer. "For my part, my brothers, I could not speak to you as I should speak to people who have the Spirit. I had to deal with you on the merely natural plane, as infants in Christ. And so I gave you milk to drink instead of solid food, for which you were not yet ready. Indeed, you are still not ready for it, for you are still on the merely natural plane. Can you not see that while there is jealousy and strife among you, you are living on the purely human level of your lower nature?" (1 Co 3, 1-3). Where the community is more open to the Spirit, there will be greater emphasis on prayer.

Second Corinthians was written towards the end of the same year (57 A.D.). In this letter he is concerned mainly with two things: first of all, with the effect his first letter had on them, and secondly with those who criticized his work as an apostle. In many different ways he brings out the love he has for them even though the letter he wrote might have seemed to them to be more of a rebuke than a letter of love. "That letter I sent you came out of great distress and anxiety; how many tears I shed as I wrote it! But I never meant to cause you pain; I wanted you rather to know the love, the more than ordinary love, that I have for you" (2 Co 2, 3-4). "Even if I did wound you by the letter I sent, I do not now regret it. I may have been sorry for it when I saw that the letter had caused you pain, even if only for a time; but now I am happy, not that your feelings were wounded but that the wound led to a change of heart" (2 Co 6, 8-9).

But the main point of the letter is to defend his authority as an apostle which apparently was being challenged by some of the critics at Corinth.

There are not many references to prayer in this letter. When they are found they are related directly or indirectly to the defense of his ministry. Even the prayerful greeting at the beginning of the letter is taken up with this thought. If he suffers in his ministry, it is to bring them salvation. If he enjoys consolation, it is to bring them comfort. "Grace and peace to you from God our Father and the Lord Jesus Christ. Praise be to the God and Father of our Lord Jesus Christ, the all-merciful Father, the God whose consolation never fails us. He comforts us in all our troubles, so that we in turn may be able to comfort others in any trouble of theirs and to share with them the consolation we ourselves received from God. As Christ's cup of suffering overflows, and we suffer with him, so also through Christ our consolation overflows. If distress be our lot, it is the price we pay for your consolation, for your salvation; if our lot be consolation, it is to help us to bring you comfort, and strength to face with fortitude the same sufferings we now endure" (2 Co 1, 2-7).

He asks for their prayers that God will deliver him from the perils he undergoes in the service of Christ and the flock. "In saying this, we should like you to know, dear friends, how serious was the trouble that came upon us in the province of Asia . . . . From such mortal peril God delivered us; and he will deliver us again, he on whom our hope is fixed. Yes, he will continue to deliver us, if you will co-operate by praying for us. Then, with so many people praying for our deliverance, there will be many to give thanks on our behalf for the gracious favor God has shown toward us" (2 Co 1, 8-11).

There follows a passage which is most illuminating to bring home the meaning of Christian prayer. Again he is defending his ministry. His hearers might call in question the sincerity of his desire to come to them. He tells them that he is sincere and draws a comparison between his own sincerity in desiring to come to them and God's sincerity in fulfilling his promises. These promises are all fulfilled in Christ. He is, therefore, God's Yes to all of the promises. For this reason when we give glory to God, it is through Christ, because he is the one in whom all of God's promises have been fulfilled. "As God is true, the language in which we address you is not an ambiguous blend of Yes and No. With him it was, and is, Yes. He is the Yes pronounced upon God's promises, every one of them. That is why, when we give glory to God, it is through Christ Jesus that we say 'Amen' " (2 Co 1, 18-21). All of the glory which is given to God is given through Christ. This makes the prayer of the Christian different from any other prayer. Those promises are not yet complete in us, but we have been given the pledge of the perfect fulfilment through the gift of the Spirit. "It is God also who has set his seal upon us, and as a pledge of what is to come has given the Spirit to dwell in our hearts" (2 Co 1, 22).

His very sufferings in the ministry become an occasion for the prayer of thanksgiving. He compares himself to a prisoner who is part of the triumphal procession of his conqueror. Ordinarily such a procession would hardly be an occasion for thanks. But this is no ordinary procession. It is Christ's triumphal procession. Those who march in it are not bearing witness to a human conquest. They are revealing the design of God himself. "Thanks be to God, who continually leads us about, captives in Christ's triumphal procession, and everywhere uses us to reveal and spread abroad the fragrance of the knowledge of himself" (2 Co 2, 14).

He takes the occasion to speak about the special gift of prayer which God had given to him. Again, he does this in order to establish his position as a special minister of God and Christ. "I am obliged to boast. It does no good; but I shall go on to tell of visions and revelations granted by the Lord. I know a Christian man who fourteen years ago (whether in the body or out of it, I do not know—God knows) was caught up as far as the third heaven. And I know that this same man (whether in the body or out of it, I do not know—God knows) was caught up into paradise, and heard words so secret that human lips may not repeat them" (2 Co 12, 1-5). This experience must have taken place sometime before his first missionary journey. It was something he never forgot. He recalls it as if it were only yesterday. He was privileged with other visions and revelations which he does not mention here (cf. Ac 9, 3; 16, 9; 18, 9; 22, 17-18; 27, 23. Ga 1, 16; 2, 2). However, this experience surpassed all the others. What is obvious is that Paul was given an extraordinary gift of prayer which on occasion became ecstatic, so that he did not know whether he still remained in his body or not.

The only passage concerning prayer which is not related to the defense of his ministry is the one which has to do with the collection for God's people. Though their generosity would be a great relief to the need of God's people, that would not be the only or the greatest effect. The greater result would be the prayer of thanksgiving that would be offered. "Through our action such generosity will issue in thanksgiving to God, for as a piece of willing service this is not only a contribution toward the needs of God's people; more than that, it overflows in a flood of thanksgiving to God. For through the proof which this affords, many will give honor to God when they see how humbly you obey him and how faithfully you confess the gospel of Christ; and will thank him for your liberal contribution to their need and to the general good. And as they join in prayer on your behalf, their hearts will go out to you because of the richness of the grace which God has imparted to

you. Thanks be to God for his gift beyond words" (2 Co
9, 11-15).

In the conclusion of the letter Paul makes all that he
has said in the letter an object of his prayer. He does not
want to hurt them. At the same time he wants them to
come to understand his own mission in a more Christian
way, so that there would be peace among them. This is
what he now puts in the form of a prayer. "Our prayer
to God is that we may not have to hurt you; we are not
concerned to be vindicated ourselves; we want you to
do what is right, even if we should seem to be discred-
ited. For we have no power to act against the truth but
only for it. We are well content to be weak at any time
if only you are strong. Indeed, my whole prayer is that
all may be put right with you" (2 Co 13, 7-9).

He concludes by urging them to live in peace. This
will take place if they live in fellowship through the gift
of fellowship which comes from the Holy Spirit. "Mend
your ways; take our appeal to heart; agree with one
another; live in peace; and the God of love and peace
will be with you. Greet one another with the kiss of
peace . . . . . The grace of the Lord Jesus Christ, and the
love of God, and fellowship in the Holy Spirit, be with
you all" (2 Co 13, 11-14).

In Second Corinthians, then, the references to prayer
are mostly concerned with the defense of his ministry.
This gives him occasion to praise God for the consolation he grants in his suffering (1, 3). It also prompts him
to ask for their prayers for his continued deliverance (1,
11). In a very striking passage he mentions that when we
give glory to God we do it through Christ (1, 21). His
sufferings even become an occasion for thanksgiving be-

cause they serve to reveal God (2, 14). He speaks of the extraordinary gift of prayer which has been given to him, which should attest his authority as an apostle (12, 1-5). He looks upon the prayer that results from the money they are giving to God's people as a greater result than satisfying their physical needs (9, 11-15). He concludes with the prayer that all will be put right with them (13, 9).

(c) The Letter To The Galatians (57 A.D.)

We do not find many references to prayer in this letter. What we do find, however, is important. Paul wrote the letter to warn the Galatians against the re-introduction of the practices of the Mosaic Law. He emphasizes the fact that they have been redeemed by Christ and have received a new Spirit, the Spirit of sonship. They have become new creatures in Christ. Therefore they should not return to anything that belongs to the old creation, not even to the Law.

What Paul has to say on prayer in this letter comes from the particular orientation of the letter.

He begins with his usual greeting, emphasizing that it is Christ who has sacrificed himself for our sins. He wastes no time in pointing out that our justification comes from Christ, not from the Law. The very mention of Christ's sacrifice brings a prayer of praise to Paul's lips. "Grace and peace to you from God the Father and our Lord Jesus Christ, who sacrificed himself for our sins, to rescue us out of this present age of wickedness, as our God and Father willed: to whom be glory forever and ever. Amen" (Ga 1, 3-5).

It is interesting that Paul proves his point from the very nature of their prayer as Christians. He wants to show that the gospel has brought what the Law could never bring. Through the gospel and our faith we have become sons with the Son. The Law did not bring worship. It simply prepared us for this. When the time came, "God sent his own Son, born of a woman, born under the Law, to purchase freedom for the subjects of the Law, in order that we might attain the status of sons" (Ga 4, 4-5). The proof of this is our prayer when we say "Father." We could not say this unless we were given the Spirit of the Son. "To prove that you are sons, God has sent into our hearts the Spirit of his Son, crying 'Abba! Father!' You are therefore no longer a slave but a son, and if a son, then also by God's own act an heir" (Ga 4, 6-7).

The Spirit who gives us the power to say "Father" should direct our lives. This means that he should direct our lives as sons. Paul describes how the lower nature wars against this life of the Spirit. Though he does not say this directly, it could be inferred that our lower nature also wars against the life of prayer. He describes the characteristics of a person whose life is led by the Spirit. Again, he does not describe prayer as one of these; but it is difficult to see how these characteristics could be found in a person who does not pray. "The harvest of the Spirit is love, joy, peace, patience, kindness, goodness, fidelity, gentleness, and self-control. There is no law dealing with such things as these. And those who belong to Christ Jesus have crucified the lower nature with its passions and desires. If the Spirit is the source of our life, let the Spirit also direct our course" (Ga 5, 22-25).

Though, as we see, there is not a great deal concerning prayer in Galatians, one major point stands out: it is the Spirit who enables us to pray in the way that is characteristically Christian. Paul stressed the role of the Spirit because of his purpose in the letter which was to oppose the re-introduction of the practices of Judaism. It is the Spirit who gives us sonship, liberates us from the Law, and enables us to say what we are, that we are sons in confessing God as our Father. It is the Spirit who brings that harvest of blessings, which are the plentitude of grace and the fulfilment of all the messianic promises.

d. The Letter To The Romans (58 A.D.)

Paul wrote this letter to the Romans while he was visiting the church at Corinth in the year 58 A.D. The theme of the letter is essentially the same as that found in Galatians. He is chiefly concerned with the meaning of the new life they have as Christians. The distinctiveness of this new life is seen in the nature of faith. For this reason most of what Paul says has to do with an exposition of the meaning of Christian faith and how it affects this new life. His tone is more serene in this letter than in the others, though the feeling is just as intense and the thought as vigorous.

He does not waste any time in coming to the point. Early in the first chapter he describes the central importance of faith. "For I am not ashamed of the Gospel. It is the saving power for everyone who has faith—the Jew first, but the Greek also— because here is revealed God's way of righting wrong, a way that starts from faith and ends in faith; as Scripture says, 'he shall gain life who is justified through faith' " (Rom 1, 16-17).

The meaning of Christian faith is brought out in the course of the letter largely through comparison and contrast. He compares the Gentile converts with the Jewish converts to show that neither has the right to lord it over the other, since they are all justified through faith. He contrasts the condition of those who do have faith with those who do not—the Gentiles, the unconverted Jews, and in general all men who are joined with Adam in solidarity of sin and death.

This exposition of the meaning of the Christian life is at the same time a reflection on the history of God's merciful dealing with mankind. The climax of God's action is the redemption, in which we participate through the gift of the Spirit and faith. While Paul is reflecting on this history, he is suddenly overwhelmed with the mystery of it all. He cannot contain himself. His wonder bursts out in spontaneous prayers of praise. More of these doxologies occur in this letter than in any of the others.

We find the usual prayer in this greeting to them. "I send greetings to all of you in Rome whom God loves and has called to be his dedicated people. Grace and peace to you from God our Father and the Lord Jesus Christ. Let me begin by thanking my God, through Jesus Christ, for you all, because all over the world they are telling the story of your faith. God is my witness, the God to whom I offer the humble service of my spirit by preaching the gospel of his Son: God knows how continually I make mention of you in my prayers, and am always asking that by his will I may, somehow or other, succeed at long last in coming to visit you" (Rm 1, 7-10). He offers his thanks, then, through Jesus Christ for all that God has done for them. He mentions that he prays for them very often. He prays also that he might have the chance to come to them.

In the doxologies which occur four times in the letter we find much that is instructive for Christian prayer. Such prayers of praise were part of the regular life of worship of the Jewish people. They came spontaneously to Paul's lips at the mention of certain key words or key themes.

The first occurs as Paul recalls the relationship of the pagan world with God. Instead of giving honor to God and rendering him thanks they dishonored God and debased themselves. When he mentions the word "Creator" it calls forth from him the prayer of praise. This is the kind of response the world also should have made to God the creator, but it did not. His own prayer of praise acts as a contrast to the way in which the pagan world had responded to God. "They have bartered away the true God for a false one, and have offered reverence and worship to created things instead of to the Creator, who is blessed forever; amen" (Rm 1, 25).

The second prayer occurs while he reflects on God's mysterious dealing with his own people. Throughout the letter he is at pains to show his own love for his people. He could even pray to be outcast from Christ for the sake of his brothers, his natural kinsfolk (Rm 9, 3). His deepest desire and prayer is for their salvation (Rm 10, 1). "What I want to say now is no pretence; I say it in union with Christ—it is the truth—my conscience in union with the Holy Spirit assures me of it too. What I want to say is this: my sorrow is so great, my mental anguish so endless, I would willingly be condemned and be cut off from Christ if it could help my brothers of Israel, my own flesh and blood. They were adopted as sons, they were given the glory and the covenants; the Law and the ritual were drawn up for them, and the promises were made to them. They are descended from the patriarchs and from their flesh and blood came Christ who is above all, God forever blessed! Amen" (Rm 9, 1-5).

Not all of the translations punctuate the sentence in such a way that the doxology is given to Christ. Some put it in the more traditional form, making it a separate sentence. "May God, supreme above all, be blessed forever! Amen." But both the grammatical structure and the sense seem to demand that the doxology be referred to Christ.

The third of the doxologies occurs as Paul reflects on the way in which the mystery of sin entered into the saving design of God. "For in making all mankind prisoners to disobedience, God's purpose was to show mercy to all mankind. O depth of wealth, wisdom, and knowledge in God! How unsearchable his judgments, how untraceable his ways! Who knows the mind of the Lord? Who has been his counsellor? Who has ever made a gift to him, to receive a gift in return? Source, Guide, and Goal of all that is—to him be glory forever! Amen" (Rm 11, 32-36).

In this hymn of praise Paul celebrates the whole mystery of salvation. The hymn expresses the whole meaning of the religion of Israel. There is only one God. All that exists comes from him. He is the one who directs all things to their goal. He himself is the goal of all that he does. Yet it is only when the fulness of revelation comes that the fulness of this doxology can be appreciated. Only when we realize how God in his mercy included all men in his plan of salvation can we sing that hymn of praise in a way that was never possible in the Old Testament.

This prayer helps us discover the nature of Christian prayer. Prayer of praise has a double reference. It celebrates God for what he is in himself, first of all. But this praise is also always related to what he has done in his saving acts. The praise that is given to God in the Old Testament differs from that in the New. It is always, of course, directed to the one true God. But in the New Testament there is, first of all, a greater motive for praise. We have been given in fact the complete motive for praise because we have seen the final revelation of God's saving acts. Secondly our praise is given to the Father through Christ (as will be brought out in the final doxology of this letter). The prayer of praise never abstracts from the saving deeds of God which reveal the very praiseworthiness of God. For this reason when the Christian makes use of the prayers of praise of the Old Testament, as for example the psalms, he should always pray them in another key. He is praying from a different vantage point. He is praying from within the very completeness of God's saving act. He has been drawn into this act and into this event through the gift of the Spirit. His praise has its power, its orientation, and its finality from the fact of the definitive revelation of God's love in Christ.

Both the Jews and the Gentiles have common ground for their praise of God. The Jews should praise God because the promise made to the Patriarchs was fulfilled when Christ became a servant of the Jewish people. But the Gentiles also have reason to praise God for his mercy. What was given to the Jews as a fulfilment of a promise was also given to the Gentiles out of God's loving mercy. The passage we here quote at length shows how all prayer of praise is rooted in acknowledgment of God's glory which is seen in his saving acts. "The reason Christ became the servant of circumcised Jews was not only so that God could faithfully carry out the promises made to the patriarchs, it was also to get the pagans to give glory to God for his mercy, as scripture says in one place: 'For this I shall praise you among the Gentiles and sing to your name.' And in another place: 'Rejoice, Gentiles, with his people,' and in a third place: 'Let all the Gentiles praise the Lord, let all the peoples sing his praises.' Isaiah too has this to say: 'The root of Jesse will appear, rising up to rule the lips of both Jew and Gentile. God's saving power has reached out to embrace each of them. They have common ground for praising God.

Immediately following this Paul adds a prayer of his own which resumes all of the doctrinal themes of the letter. "May the God of hope bring you such joy and peace in your faith that the power of the Holy Spirit will remove all bounds to hope" (Rm 15, 13). He is the God of hope because he is the God of love. He is particularly the God of love in the New Testament because we see there are no bounds to his love. His gift could not be greater either in degree or in its universality. The gift of his Spirit creates the same dynamism in us—to release our love and our hope.

The letter ends with a hymn of praise to God who not only called them, but will also give them the grace to perservere. "To him who has power to make your standing sure, according to the Gospel I brought you and the proclamation of Jesus Christ, according to the revelation of that divine secret kept in silence for long ages but now disclosed, and through prophetic scriptures by the eternal God's command made known to all nations, to bring them to faith and obedience—to God who alone is wise, through Jesus Christ, be glory for endless ages! Amen" (Rm 16, 25-27).

Some manuscripts place this doxology at another place in the letter. Others omit it altogether. The weight of authority favors both its authenticity and its place at the conclusion of the letter.

It is in fact characteristically Pauline. The whole contents of the letter are condensed into this prayer. There are other doxologies in Paul's letters, but none of them has the upward sweep of this one, as it condenses the whole of his message in a few dense phrases (cf. Ga 1, 5; Ep 3, 21; Ph 4, 20; I Tm 1, 17). It has all the force and compression of the finale of a symphony.

The main ideas are the following. God is the one who has the power to fulfill that which he has begun—he is the one who can give the Christians the strength to persevere in the faith. The gospel is the complete revelation of God's plan. It is the proclamation of Jesus Christ. God's design was hidden during the past but now it is completely revealed. There is continuity between the proclamation of the gospel of Jesus Christ and the prophetic utterances of the Old Testament. The goal of all of this activity is to bring men to the obedience of faith. Let glory be given to God, who in his vision conceived this and in his power carried it out, through Jesus

Christ, who is the ultimate revelation of the wisdom and power of God.

Besides what we learn from these doxologies, there are many other important points concerning Christian prayer. One of the primary lessons is the role of the Spirit: "If a man does not possess the Spirit of Christ, he is no Christian . . . .,For all who are moved by the Spirit of God are sons of God. The Spirit you have received is not a spirit of slavery leading you back into a life of fear, but a Spirit that makes us sons, enabling us to cry 'Abba! Father!' In that cry the Spirit of God joins with our spirit in testifying that we are God's children; and if children, then heirs" (Rm 8, 9, 14-17).

This is a strong expression. Another translation puts it, "The Spirit himself and our spirit bear united witness that we are children of God." We can truly pray as sons because we have the Spirit of the Son.

The gift of the Spirit, though it has made us sons, has not fully liberated us. The Spirit gives the first-fruits of the fulness of life which is to come. But we have to live in hope. This fact serves to bring out another aspect of our life of prayer. Someone might say that we do not really know what to hope for, and therefore that we do not know what to pray for. Paul says that our prayers have their certainty from the presence of the Holy Spirit in us. "For we have been saved though only in hope. Now to see is no longer to hope: why should man endure and wait for what he already sees? But if we hope for something we do not yet see, then in waiting for it, we show our endurance. In the same way the Spirit comes to the aid of our weakness. We do not even know how we ought to pray, but through our inarticulate groans the Spirit himself is pleading for us, and God who searches our inmost being knows what the Spirit means, because he pleads for God's own people in God's own way; and in everything as we know, he co-operates for good with those who love God and are called according to his purpose" (Rm 8, 24-28).

The Spirit pleads through our pleading, filling up the blind spots with his knowledge and the weaknesses with his power. The Christian never prays alone, or at the prompting of his own spirit. He prays through the prompting of the Holy Spirit. The Spirit of Christ and the spirit of man unite in one voice. This is the meaning of Christian prayer.

Paul adds another reason for hope besides the presence of the Spirit. While the Spirit of Christ is pleading within us, Christ himself is pleading for us at the right hand of the Father. "It is Christ—Christ who died and, more than that, was raised from the dead—who is at God's right hand, and indeed pleads our cause" (Rm 8, 34). The Christian then is a special object of God's love. He can hope because he is loved. Christ's own love for us continues after his resurrection. He is constantly interceding for us.

It should be noted that while the Spirit prays *with* us, Christ prays *for* us. Our own prayer takes on the characteristics that belong to the Spirit. These could be described as *depth, movement,* and *inwardness.* Our own spirit which possesses these characteristics to a limited degree takes on the depth, the movement, and the inwardness of the Spirit of God. In another place Paul describes the nature of the Spirit as the depths of God. "For the Spirit explores everything, even the depths of God's own nature. Among men, who knows what a man is but the man's own spirit within him? In the same way, only the Spirit of God knows what God is. This is the Spirit that we have received from God" (1 Co 2, 10-12). Our own prayer is caught up in the movement of the Spirit who is moving us to the fulfilment of that of which he is the pledge. It shares in the depth of the Spirit and is no longer limited to our superficial knowledge and love. It shares in the inwardness of the Spirit because the Spirit's inwardness is his relationship to the Father and to the Son. Our own prayer takes on a trinitarian character because of the presence of the Spirit. Christ's prayer for us is the prayer of one in whom the movement of the Spirit has reached its completion. His prayer flows from the fulness he possesses. It is for those who are on the way to that fulness through the presence of his Spirit.

There are a few other passages in Romans which can help us form our ideas on Christian prayer. Our prayer can help us learn the will of God so that we can do the perfect thing. In this passage Paul is directly speaking about worship. But what he says certainly includes the worship which we call prayer. "Think of God's mercy, my brothers, and worship him, I beg you, in a way that is worthy of thinking beings, by offering your living bodies as a holy sacrifice, truly pleasing to God. Do not model yourselves on the behavior of the world around you, but let your behavior change, modelled by your new mind. This is the only way to *discover the will* of God and know what is good, what it is that God wants, what is the perfect thing to do" (Rm 12, 1-2).

The idea of finding the will of God plays an important part in the teaching of St. Paul. The word which is here translated "to discover the will of God" occurs often in his letters (Rm 1, 28; 2, 18; 12, 2; 14, 22. 1 Co 3, 13; 11, 28; 16, 3, 2 Co 2, 8; 22, 13. Ga 6, 4; Ep 5, 10; Ph 1, 10. 1 Th 2, 4; 5, 21. 1 Tm 3, 10). There are various nuances to the word, but basically it always involves a critical judgment in what pertains to salvation. It can be God's own judgment concerning man's disposition, or man's critical discernment of God's will. There is discernment which belongs to the final age, the age of the Spirit. This is the discernment which belongs to the Christian because of the gift of the Spirit. It is this type of discernment described in the test quoted above, "This is the only way to discover the will of God and know what is good, what it is that God wants, what is the perfect thing to do." It is also brought out in other places. *"Make sure what would have the Lord's approval;* take no part in the barren deeds of darkness, but show them up for what they are" (Ep 5, 10-11). "Examine yourselves: are you living the life of faith? *Put yourselves to the test"* (2 Co 13, 5). "And this is my prayer, that your love may grow ever richer and richer in knowledge and insight of every kind, and may thus bring you the gift of *true discrimination"* (Ph 1, 10). "Do not stifle inspiration, and do not despise prophetic utterances, but *bring them all to the test* and then keep what is good in them and avoid the bad of whatever kind" (1 Th 5, 21). *"A man must test himself* before eating his share of the bread and drinking from the cup" (1 Co 11, 28).

The particular power of discernment which belongs to the Christian is contrasted with that which belongs to the Jew. Speaking of the Jews, Paul says, "But as for you—you bear the name of Jew; you rely upon the law and are proud of your God; you know his will; *you are aware of moral distinctions* because you receive instruction from the law" (Rm 2, 17-18). The Jews have a power of discernment which comes from the Law which was given to them. But the Christians have a special power that comes from the gift of the Spirit. They have need for greater discernment because with the fulness of the gift there is also an invitation to the fullest possible response.

There can be no doubt that prayer has an important place in this critical discernment of the will of God. The entire life of the Christian is to be lived as a sacrifice in the presence of God. Through this kind of an offering he will be able to discern the will of God. But prayer is the privileged moment within this entire life. It is this privileged moment which becomes the moment of truth, the moment of critical discernment, since it is in an especial way the moment of listening.

One of the favorite themes of St. Paul is the fact that we should thank God in everything that we do for all that he has done for us. This is such a spontaneous and constant refrain in Paul's letters that it could only come from an habitual disposition to see everything in the light of God's gift. In this letter this theme of gratitude is present, though it occurs only in a few passages. He begins the letter with a prayer of thanks. "First I thank my God through Jesus Christ for all of you and for the way in which your faith is spoken of all over the world" (Rm 1, 8). One of the signs of the corruption of the pagan world is that they refused to give God thanks. "Knowing God, they have refused to honor him as God, or to render him thanks" (Rm 1, 21). He uses the fact that each Christian gives thanks to God when he is eating, no matter whether he is eating food allowed to a Jew or not allowed, to show that such dietary laws are not important. "He who eats meat has the Lord in mind when he eats, since he gives thanks to God; and he who abstains has the Lord in mind no less, since he too gives thanks to God" (Rm 14, 6). The fact that each one can give thanks to the Lord shows that the action of eating is of one piece with all other Christian actions. They all belong to the Lord. Paul goes on to say, "For no one of us lives, and equally no one of us dies for himself alone. If we live, we live for the Lord; and if we die, we die for the Lord. Whether therefore we live or die, we belong to the Lord" (Rm 14, 7-8).

Finally Paul asks for the prayers of the Christians in Rome. He asks them to pray that he may be preserved from harm, and that his mission to the Christians in Jerusalem may succeed. He sees them as his helpers in the apostolate through their prayers for him. "I implore you by our Lord Jesus Christ and by the love that the Spirit inspires, be my allies in the fight; pray to God for me that I may be saved from unbelievers in Judea and that my errand to Jerusalem may find acceptance with God's people, so that by his will I may come to you in a happy frame of mind and enjoy a time of rest with you. The God of peace be with you all. Amen" (Rm 15, 30-33).

There are two main ideas which we learn from the Letter to the Romans concerning Christian prayer. The first is the importance of the prayer of praise. This is seen in the recurring doxologies in the letter. The progressive revelation of God's ways of dealing with mankind in the history of salvation calls forth the prayer of praise on the lips of St. Paul. Another important poii ¿ is the role of the Holy Spirit in Christian prayer. Because we have the gift of the Spirit we can pray as sons. The Spirit joins himself to our spirit, pleads with us, fills up what is lacking in our prayer, orders what is disordered, making it truly what it is—the prayer of a son. While the Spirit is pleading *with* us, Christ is at the right hand of the Father pleading *for* us.

We also saw (largely by way of inference) the important place that prayer has for the discernment of the will of God. If the ordering of our lives through opening ourselves to the Spirit allows us to discern God's will, then it is evident that the deliberate and conscious ordering that takes place in prayer is a privileged moment for discerning God's will. Finally we saw how the theme of gratitude recurs, an attitude of mind which conditions the whole of one's life.

e. The Letter To The Philipians (56-57 A.D.)

The Philippians were to Paul what John was to Jesus, the beloved disciple. This was the first Christian community he had founded on European soil. Paul had a great affection for them. He wrote the letter to thank them for the contributions they had made to his livelihood and to encourage them to grow in their appreciation of the common life they shared in Christ. This conviction of their common fellowship with him and one another in Christ receives great emphasis in this letter. As might be expected, the remarks on prayer in this letter are also related to this notion of fellowship. His prayer for them arises out of this fellowship. It is a prayer that this very fellowship be deepened and continue to grow.

The whole tone of the letter is that of Christian friendship. This is seen to have a passion and a depth which distinguish it from anything that is merely human. It is not simply a warmed up or warmed over human friendship, nor is it the winter light which often passes for charity, where there is brightness but no warmth. The relationship of grace has made even more human that relationship which we call friendship and evoked greater expressions of love and ardent desire for even greater fellowship with one another in Christ.

He begins his letter by reminding them of their bond with one another through their union with Christ. "From Paul and Timothy, servants of Christ Jesus, to all those of God's people, *incorporate* in Christ Jesus, who live at Philippi" (Ph 1, 1). They should be united in their defense of the faith. "Contend *as one man* for the gospel faith" (Ph 2, 28). They share the same struggle. "You and I are *engaged in the same contest*" (Ph 1, 30). They have a common life because they share in the same Spirit. The happiness and joy which comes from the union of their own lives overflows to Paul also, who shares their life. "If then our *common life in Christ* yields anything to stir the heart, any loving consolations, any *sharing of the Spirit*, any warmth of affection or compassion, fill up my cup with happiness by *thinking and feeling alike, with the same love for one another, the same turn of mind, and a common care for unity*" (Ph 2, 1-2). He tells them the source of this unity, the life they have in Christ. "Let your bearing towards one another arise out of your life in Christ Jesus" (Ph 2, 5).

They are one because they worship the same Lord and belong to the same Lord. It is he who brought about the fellowship through his redemptive death. "For the divine nature was his from the first; yet he did not think to snatch at equality with God, but made himself nothing, assuming the nature of a slave. Bearing the human likeness, revealed in human shape, he humbled himself, and in obedience accepted even death— death on a cross. Therefore God raised him to the heights and bestowed on him the name above all names, that at the name of Jesus every knee should bow—in heaven, on earth, and in the depths—and every tongue confess, " 'Jesus Christ is Lord', to the glory of God the Father" (Ph 2, 6-11).

Because of this fellowship with one another they will be his pride on the Day of Christ. They will be his proof that he did not run his race in vain or work in vain (Ph 2, 16). They share a common sacrificial life and a common joy. Their life of faith is their sacrifice. Perhaps Paul's sacrifice will involve the shedding of his blood. In any case they are one in their sacrifice; they are also one in their joy. "But if my life-blood is to crown that sacrifice which is the offering up of your faith, I am glad of it, and I *share* my gladness with you all. Rejoice, you no less than I, and let us *share* our joy" (Ph 2, 17-18).

It is this bond with Christ which outweighs all other things. "I look on everything as so much rubbish if only I can have Christ and find myself incorporate in him" (Ph 3, 8). This sharing in the life of Christ means also a sharing in his suffering. "All I care for is to know Christ, to experience the power of his resurrection from the dead" (Ph 3, 10-11).

Turning our attention more explicitly to prayer, we observe that there are not many remarks in this letter directly connected with prayer. Where they do occur it is the notion of fellowship which is emphasized, the fellowship they have with one another, arising from their common life in Christ.

He begins the letter with his usual prayer of thanks. Here he expresses his thanks to God for the share they have had in the spreading of the gospel. He describes his own love for them, and shows how this love expresses itself in prayer for them. "I thank my God whenever I think of you; and when I pray for you all, my prayers are always joyful, because of the part you have taken in the work of the gospel . . . . God knows how I long for you all, with the deep yearning of Christ Jesus himself. And this is my prayer, that your love may grow ever richer and richer in knowledge and insight of every kind, and may thus bring you the gift of true discernment. Then on the Day of Christ you will be flawless and without blame, reaping the full harvest of righteousness that comes through Jesus Christ, to the glory and praise of God" (Ph 1, 8-11).

What are the objects of Paul's prayer for them? To comment on these would take a treatise. What Paul prays for takes in the whole of his desire for them. He prays first of all for that gift which comprises all of the other gifts, the gift of love. The word which he uses is the one word which sums up the meaning of the Christian life, the word *agape*. He asks not only that they might love, but that their love might be like a river which overflows its banks. But the love he is speaking of is not simply a feeling or a sentiment. It shows its genu-

157

inity in discernment, insight, good sense. This in turn will lead them to register the movement of the Spirit by judging what is the better thing to do. All of this prepares them to stand in the presence of Christ when he comes. They will stand in his presence because their lives are sincere, flawless, and there is found nothing worthy of blame. They will reap the fulness of the fruit of their union with Christ. And all of this resounds to the glory and praise of God. We find here a comprehensive description of the object of Christian prayer, taking in the relationship the Christian has to Christ, to one another, and to the Father. The prayer itself is a manifestation of the very *agape* which is the object of Paul's petition for them. Because his own love overflows, and because it gives him the power to discern God's will, he can pray for the Phillippians in this way.

Their bond with one another is shown in their prayer for one another. Paul tells them how much he profits from their prayer for him. The strength which he needs in his trials comes from their prayer for him and from the presence of Christ's Spirit within him. "Yes, I will rejoice, knowing well that the issue of it all will be my deliverance, because you are praying for me and the Spirit of Jesus Christ is given me for support" (Ph 1, 19).

He tells them further that if they have any need whatever they should pray for it. Their prayer of petition should be accompanied by the prayer of thanksgiving. "The Lord is near; have no anxiety, but in everything make your requests known to God in prayer and petition with thanksgiving. Then the peace of God, which is beyond our utmost understanding, will keep guard over your hearts and your thoughts, in Christ Jesus" (Ph 4, 6-7). We see here another effect of Christian prayer, the gift of peace. Christian life should not be a life of tortured anxiety. It should be a life of peace which envelopes our hearts and thoughts. This life of peace is another name for a life in Christ Jesus.

When he thinks of the abundance of God's gifts to them, he cannot help but express this in a doxology. As we saw, these prayers of praise are particularly appropriate when he recalls the great love of God in his saving deeds. Most of these doxologies occur in the Epistle to the Romans; but the doxology here is of the same nature. He is thanking them for their generosity to him in sending him a gift of money. This reminds him of God's own generosity. This in turn evokes a spontaneous exclamation of praise. "I am paid in full, now that I have received from Epaphroditus what you sent. It is a fragrant offering, an acceptable sacrifice, pleasing to God. And my God will supply all your wants out of the magnificence of his riches in Christ Jesus. To our God and Father be glory for endless ages! Amen" (Ph 4, 18-20).

The letter ends with a prayer for them. "The grace of our Lord Jesus Christ be with your Spirit" (Ph 4, 23). It is a prayer for union, that their own spirit, their own lives, might be ruled by the presence of Christ with them and in them. This sums up his desire for them and his love for them.

By way of summary, we can say that the Epistle to the Phillipians brings out a special aspect of Christian prayer. It is rooted in union and leads to deeper union. This union is described in different ways—sharing the same life, incorporated in the same Christ, having the same Lord, worshipping the same Lord, thinking and feeling alike, sharing the same joy, and sharing the same suffering. We find that prayer is to Christian fellowship what speech is to lovers or what words are to the poet. The fellowship expresses itself in the desire to deepen the fellowship, to bring it to fruition. This desire becomes alive when it begins to speak. This speaking is prayer.

f. Letter To The Ephesians (61-63 A.D.)

The Letter to the Ephesians provides us with all the elements necessary to form a theology of prayer according to Pauline thought. At the same time it combines many of the themes which appear in the other letters: the mystery of God hidden from all ages and revealed in Christ through whom we are justified by faith. (Romans); the mystery of Christ who is the image of the invisible God, the embodiment of the deity, and the first fruits of the dead (Colossians); the mystery of the communion which unites us to one another and to Christ (Phillippians); the role of the Spirit in our lives and in a particular way in our prayer (Galatians, Corinthians).

Ephesians, however, has its own particular emphasis. This emphasis is on the Church as the concrete realization of God's grace and of his eternal design to unite all men in Christ. What Paul says about prayer is related to this emphasis on the Church as the focal point of the fulfilment of God's design.

He begins with the usual salutation in which he asks for grace and peace from God the Father and from Christ. "Grace to you and peace from God our Father and the Lord Jesus Christ" (Ep 1, 2). Then he goes on to describe how their calling, their vocation, has its origin in God's free gift. He does not do this in an abstract way but in the context of a prayer of praise to God for the marvels of his wisdom and his love. "Praise be to the God and Father of our Lord Jesus Christ, who has bestowed on us in Christ every spiritual blessing in the heavenly realms. In Christ he chose us before the world was founded, to be dedicated, to be without blemish in his sight, to be full of love; and he destined us—such was his will and pleasure—to be accepted as his sons through Jesus Christ, that the glory of his gracious gift, so graciously bestowed on us in his Beloved, might resound to his praise. For in Christ our release is secured and our sins are forgiven through the shedding of his blood: therein lies the richness of God's free grace lavished upon us, imparting full wisdom and insight. He has made known to us his hidden purpose—such was his will and pleasure determined beforehand in Christ—to be put into effect when the time was ripe: namely, that the universe, and all in heaven and on earth, might be brought into unity in Christ" (Ep 1, 3–10). In a few verses he gives the whole basis for the Christian prayer of praise— the Father's choice of us, and the fulfilment of his choice through the redemptive activity of Christ.

He stresses the fact that it is God's doing, his gift, his choice. "It is by his grace you are saved. And in union with Christ Jesus he raised us up and enthroned us with him in the heavenly realms, so that he might display in the ages to come how immense are the resources of his grace, and how great his kindness to us in Christ Jesus. For it is by his grace you are saved, through trusting in him; it is not your own doing. It is God's gift, not a reward for work done. There is nothing for anyone to boast of. For we are God's work of art, created in Christ Jesus, to devote ourselves to the good deeds for which God has designed us" (Ep 2, 5-10).

His own gifts as an apostle are no less gift and grace than the gifts they have received. "Such is the gospel of which I was made a minister, by God's gift, bestowed unmerited on me in the working of his power. To me, who am less than the least of all God's people, he has granted of his grace the privilege of proclaiming to the Gentiles the good news of the unfathomable riches of Christ" (Ep 3, 7-8). Each one of the Christian community has received his own gift from Christ. "But each of us has been given his gift, his due portion of Christ's bounty" (Ep 4, 7).

The grace of God in Christ is given in order to bring about a new creation. This new creation is the church. "It [the hidden purpose of God] was hidden for long ages in God the creator of the universe, in order that now, through the church, the wisdom of God in all its varied forms might be made known to the rulers and authorities in the realms of heaven. This is in accord with his age-long purpose, which he achieved in Christ Jesus our Lord" (Ep 3, 10-11).

The thought of God's grace and the power which translates grace into a living community leads Paul to a spontaneous exclamation of praise in the form of a doxology. "Now to him who is able to do immeasureably more than all we can ask or conceive, by the power which is at work among us, to him be glory in the church and in Christ Jesus from generation to generation evermore! Amen" (Ep 3, 20-21).

If God's gifts have as their origin his love freely given, they have as their term the institution and constant vitalization of the church. "And these were his gifts: some to be apostles, some prophets, some evangelists, some pastors and teachers, to equip God's people for work in his service, to the building up of the body of Christ. So shall we all at last attain to the unity inherent in our faith and our knowledge of the Son of God—to mature manhood, measured by nothing less than the full stature of Christ" (Ep 4, 11-13). When the fulness of the gifts of God is dispensed, this will be the state of maturity in Christ. The fulness is already present in Christ, but it is to be dispensed to his body, the church. "He has put everything in subjection beneath his feet, and appointed him as supreme head to the church, which is his body and as such holds within it the fulness of him who himself receives the entire fulness of God" (Ep 1, 22-23). This fulness is to be realized when they open their hearts and minds to grasp the meaning of Christ's love. "With deep roots and firm foundations, may you be strong to grasp, with all God's people, what is the breadth and length and height and depth of love of Christ, and to know it, though it is beyond knowledge. So may you attain to fulness of being, the fulness of God himself" (Ep 3, 18-19).

This union of Christ with the church is a mysterious one. It is brought about through his purifying and uniting love. He does not find the community and then adopt it; rather he makes the community by purifying it and making it his spouse. Paul uses the image of marriage to express this union of Christ and the church. "Christ also loved the church and gave himself up for it, to consecrate it, cleansing it by water and word, so that he might present the church to himself all glorious, with no stain or wrinkle or anything of the sort, but holy and without blemish. In loving his wife a man loves himself. For no one ever hated his own body: on the contrary, he provides and cares for it; and that is how Christ treats the church, because it is his body, of which we are living parts. Thus it is that (in the words of Scripture) 'a man shall leave his father and mother and shall be joined to his wife, and the two shall become a single body'. It is a great truth that is hidden here. I for my part refer it to Christ and to the church" (Ep 5, 25-32). The love which leads to union and sustains it, rendering it permanent, self-sacrificing and fruitful — this finds its most complete expression in the love of Christ for the church. Further, the love of Christ for the church is the cause of all true love, as its source, exemplar, and goal.

When we combine the understanding of the richness of God's grace together with the way this grace is realized in time, that is, in the church, we have the framework for the theology of prayer.

The Christian can pray because he has complete access to the Father. He is united with Christ and has his Spirit. For this reason the avenue to the Father is completely open. He can enter into the presence of the Father because he is united to the Son and moved by the Spirit. He can speak with confidence, freely, even boldly, knowing that he is doing so not as a stranger but as an adopted son. "For through him [Christ] we both alike [Gentile and Jew] have access to the Father in one Spirit" (Ep 2, 18). "In him we have access to God with *freedom*, in the confidence born of trust in him" (Ep 3,

12-13). This can be done through the Spirit who is given us. "And you too when you had heard the message of the truth, the good news of your salvation, and had believed it, became incorporate in Christ and received the seal of the promised Holy Spirit; and that Spirit is the pledge that we shall enter upon our heritage, when God has redeemed what is his own, to his praise and glory" (Ep 1, 13-14).

In one of the verses quoted above, St. Paul uses a favorite word to describe a characteristic of the life of the Christian. It is the word "freedom", which has been italicized in the verse in order to set it off from the other words. The Greek word is *parrhesia*. It occurs frequently in the letters of Paul. It is also found frequently in the Johannine writings. (cf. for example: 2 Co 3, 12; 7, 4. Ep 3, 12. 6,19. Ph 1,20; Col 2, 15; 1 Tm 3, 13; Phm 8. Heb 3, 6; 4. 16; 10, 19; 10, 35. 1 Jn 2, 25; 3, 21; 4, 17; 5, 14). The word is translated in a variety of ways, "boldness," "frankness," "confidence," "trust," "freedom," "openness," "constancy." The word can be used to denote either a characteristic of temperament without any specifically religious connotation, or it can be used to point out a new quality that belongs to the life of the Christian.

The new characteristic that belongs to the Christian comes from a radical transformation of his life through grace. Because he has been given the gift of the Spirit and in this way has entered into the new creation that belongs to the final age, he is a "bold creature." This does not mean that he is brash or presumptuous. It means that he can speak with freedom, boldness, frankness, confidence, constancy, because he has been drawn by grace into a new relationship, which is that of an adopted son. He has free access to the Father because there is nothing between him and the Father. The way is open. He does not have to hesitate. He cannot ask too much. The limit of the asking is determined by the limits of Christ's riches, and these are unfathomable.

The same boldness belongs to the preaching of the Christian message. It is God's word, his final word. There is no further word to come in the sense that this word awaits a further dispensation, or a further covenant. Hence the message can be preached with full confidence. This confidence comes not only from the nature of the message itself. It is rooted in the empowering Spirit who is given to the Christian.

We can learn a great deal about the meaning of Christian prayer when we examine Paul's own prayer. In the petitions which he makes for the Christians we find that very *parrhesia* operative which knows no limits in its desire. "I never cease to give thanks for you when I mention you in my prayers. I pray that the God of our Lord Jesus Christ, the all-glorious Father, may give you the spiritual powers of wisdom and vision, by which there comes the knowledge of him. I pray that your inward eyes may be illumined, so that you may know what is the hope to which he calls you, what the wealth and glory of the share he offers you among his people in their heritage, and how vast the resources of his power open to us who trust in him" (Ep 1, 16-18).

There is another description of the scope of his prayer for them. It comes after he has spoken about the freedom that the Christian has to approach God. "This, then, is what I pray, kneeling before the Father, from whom every family, whether spiritual or natural, takes

166

its name. Out of his infinite glory, may he give you the power through his Spirit for your hidden self to grow strong, so that Christ may live in your hearts through faith, and then, planted in love and built on love, you will with all the saints have strength to grasp the breadth and the length, the height and the depth; until, knowing the love of Christ, which is beyond all knowledge, you are filled with the utter fulness of God" (Ep 3, 14-19).

As is so often the case, we feel that it would take a treatise to comment on the gifts of grace for which Paul prays. It will help to point out some of the characteristics of this prayer.

First of all it is fully Christian prayer. This is so because it is Trinitarian. What forms the living framework of the prayer is faith, faith in the Father from whom all things take their origin, faith in the Spirit who is given to us, faith in the love of Christ who gave himself for us. Paul prays that the Father may give them strength and power through his gift of the Spirit. This power will enable them to open themselves to the presence of Christ through faith. Their lives, if Christ lives in them, will be totally the construction of love. Love is both the soil in which their lives are planted and from which they grow. Love is also the foundation on which the whole fabric of their lives is built. If their lives are such, they will be able to grasp what is humanly speaking unfathomable, the extent of the love of Christ. This is tantamount to saying that they will be filled with God's own fulness. This is the ultimate term of Christian faith, and it is the complete object of Paul's prayer for them. This fulness is already present in Christ. If the Christian opens himself to Christ through the power of the Spirit, this fulness will also be given to him insofar as he can share it.

This is also an appropriate place to say something about the posture in prayer. Paul speaks of praying as he kneels before the Father. It is normal that the whole person show forth his inner attitude in prayer. For this reason we find in Scripture (and for that matter in all religious worship) that the bodily actions, gestures, or posture show forth in a concrete way the disposition of the creature who is consciously putting himself in the presence of his creator. There were three postures which expressed the prayerful relationship of the Israelite (and the Christian) to God. Standing was the normal posture (Mt 6, 5; Mk 11, 25; Lk 18, 11). Kneeling was also common (Lk 22, 41; Ac 7, 60; 21, 5-6; Ep 3, 14). Special intensity of prayer was manifested in prostration (Mk 14, 35). Luke describes Christ as kneeling during his agony in the garden. Mark speaks of him as prostrating himself. There were other bodily gestures which were appropriate—the bowing of the head, raising of the hands in a gesture of supplication, casting down one's eyes and striking the breast as a sign of sorrow. All of these bodily actions are symbolic of the inner disposition of the one who is addressing God in prayer. They are consistent with a Hebrew and Christian view of man who is enfleshed spirit. The flesh must show forth in time and space that which the Spirit is expressing inwardly, if prayer is to be the expression of the whole man.

Paul exhorts the Christians to lead prayerful lives. "Let the Holy Spirit fill you: speak to one another in psalms, hymns, and songs; sing and make music in your hearts to the Lord; and in the name of our Lord Jesus Christ give thanks everyday for everything to our God and Father" (Ep 5, 18-20). "Give yourselves wholly to prayer and entreaty; pray on every occasion in the power of the Spirit. To this end keep watch and persevere, always interceding for all God's people; and pray for me, that I may be granted the right words when I open my mouth, and may boldly and freely make known his hidden purpose, for which I am an ambassador—in chains. Pray that I may speak of it boldly, as it is my duty to speak" (Ep 6, 18-20).

We find once again the elements of Christian prayer. It is Trinitarian, coming from the presence of the Spirit who moves us to pray, offered in the name of the Lord Jesus Christ to the Father. It is characterized by joy and thanksgiving. It is a prayer that first of all is sung in the heart and then on one's lips. Their prayer should be constant, not letting an occasion go by which is not sanctified by prayer. They should pray for all of God's people. He asks them to pray for him also that he may have wisdom and courage—wisdom to speak the right words, and courage to speak the message with boldness. Prayer is seen to be the warp and woof of Christian life, proceeding from the communion which they have in the Spirit, and seeking deeper union in the same Spirit. The kingdom of God depends on their prayer. Paul's own apostolate depends on their prayer for him. The whole life of the Christian is one of communion and cooperation. The communion is the sharing in the same life and the cooperation takes place in the work of the apostolate, the spreading of the Good News.

Paul concludes his letter with a prayer for them.

"May God the Father and the Lord Jesus Christ grant peace, love and faith to all the brothers. May grace and eternal life be with all who love our Lord Jesus Christ" (Ep 6, 23-24). His prayer for them comprises all of the gifts which the Father has given in Christ Jesus—peace, love, faith, grace, eternal life. These have been granted to the brothers, that is, to the church, to those who love Christ.

From this brief treatment we can see that there are in Ephesians all of the elements for a theology of prayer. There is first of all the theme of grace with all of the various nuances which this has for Paul—God's free choice of them, his gifts to them, their own new life which is the embodiment of God's gifts, the brotherhood of those who are united in Christ. It is this brotherhood which shows forth God's hidden design, which in turn is effective in drawing others into this design, "God's work of art" (Ep 2, 10).

We can find the essential characteristics of Christian prayer both in the way Paul himself prays, and in his exhortations to the Christians. Paul's prayer is first of all Trinitarian, seeking the answer to all of his prayer from the Father, in the name of the Son, through the power of the Spirit. He prays with the boldness and confidence that comes from the free access he has to the Father. There are no more curtains which separate the Father from men if one belongs to the brotherhood. His own prayer instructs us in the objects of Christian prayer. These are the gifts which foster closer union with one another, with Christ, and with the Father. Prayer is aimed at fulness—that fulness which is already in Christ, a fulness ready to be dispensed to men if they dispose themselves to receive it. The Christians are exhorted to pray for one another and for Paul in his apostolate. They should pray outwardly and also in their hearts, with gratitude and with joy. Prayer is to form the very atmosphere of their lives. There is no occasion which is not sanctified by the presence of that atmosphere, because that atmosphere is ultimately and most fundamentally the Spirit who enters each action of their lives.

(7) The Letter To The Colossians (61—63 A.D.)

Scripture scholars are not entirely agreed on the question of the relationship of Colossians with Ephesians. But that question, along with the question of the exact date of this letter, are not of great importance for our purpose.

Paul wrote this letter while he was in prison in Rome. He had not evangelized the community at Colossae personally, but when he heard of the dangers threatening their faith he decided to write to them to warn them. There were teachers among them who were confusing them with their teaching concerning regulations of eating and drinking, the practice of asceticism, and the worship of angels.

Because of the dangers which threaten them Paul is moved to single out that aspect of Christianity which puts all of the other things in their proper perspective. This brings out the particular emphasis of this letter, the primacy of Christ.

Christ is the head of all that exists. He is the head of all that exists naturally through creation and he is the head of all that belongs to the new creation which has been effected through his redemption. In his human nature he is the image of the invisible God, and in this sense has the primacy of honor which sets him above all creatures, the first-born of all creation. He is the head of the church because he was the first to rise from the dead and because the whole church exists in and through him. God wanted the fulness of the divinity to be present in him. He is the head because he has reunited all things to the Father. These are the ideas contained in that splendid description of the reality of Christ in a passage hardly excelled for its consummate beauty and its profound Christology. "He is the image of the invisible God; his is the primacy over all created things. In him everything in heaven and on earth was created, not only things visible but also the invisible orders of thrones, sovereignties, authorities, and powers: the whole universe has been created through him and for him. And he exists before everything, and all things are held together in him. He is, moreover, the head of the body, the church. He is its origin, the first to return from the dead, to be in all things alone supreme. For in him the complete being of God, by God's own choice, came to dwell. Through him God chose to reconcile the whole universe to himself, making peace through the shedding of his blood upon the cross—to reconcile all things, whether on earth or in heaven, through him alone" (Col 1, 15-20).

The value and the truth of all things, then, comes from their relationship to Christ. Whether it is a question of regulations that belong to the Law or a question of the place of angels in the worship of the church, there is only one norm, the primacy of Christ. "From now onwards, never let anyone else decide what you should eat or drink, or whether you are to observe annual festivals, New Moons or Sabbaths. These were only pale reflections of what was coming: the reality is Christ. Do not be taken in by people who like grovelling to angels and worshipping them: people like that are always going on about some vision they have had, inflating themselves to a false importance with their worldly outlook. A man of this sort is not united to the head, and it is the head that adds strength and holds the whole body together, with all its joints and sinews—and this is the only way in which it can reach its full growth in God" (Col 2, 16-19).

The remarks here concerning prayer have much in common with what we find in the other letters. But there is a special emphasis which comes from the overall theme of the letter, the primacy of Christ, and the relationship of all things to him.

What is the prayerful response to the reality of Christ and to the relationship of the Christian to Christ? It is *gratitude*. No other letter of Paul emphasizes the notion of gratitude to the extent that we find in Colossians. This idea recurs frequently in a relatively short letter.

"Grace to you and peace from God our Father. In all our prayers to God, the Father of our Lord Jesus Christ, we *thank* him for you, because we have heard of the faith you hold in Christ Jesus, and the love you bear towards all God's people" (Col 1, 2-4). "For this reason ever since the day we heard of it, we have not ceased to pray for you. We ask God that you may receive from him all wisdom and spiritual understanding for full insight into his will, so that your manner of life may be worthy of the Lord and entirely pleasing to him. We pray that you may bear fruit in active goodness of every

kind, and grow in the knowledge of God. May he
strengthen you, in his glorious might, with ample power
to meet whatever comes with fortitude, patience, and
joy; and to give *thanks* to the Father who has made you
fit to share the heritage of God's people in the realm of
light. He rescued us from the domain of darkness and
brought us away into the kingdom of his dear Son, in
whom our release is secured and our sins forgiven" (Col
1, 9-14). "Therefore, since Jesus was delivered to you as
Christ and Lord, live your lives in union with him. Be
rooted in him; be built in him; be consolidated in the
faith you were taught; let your hearts overflow with
thankfulness" (Col 2, 6-8). "Let Christ's peace be arbi-
ter in your hearts: to this peace you were called as
members of a single body. And be filled with *gratitude*.
Let the message of Christ dwell among you in all its
richness. Instruct and admonish each other with the utmost wisdom. Sing *thankfully* in your hearts to God,
with psalms and hymns and spiritual songs. Whatever
you are doing, whether you speak or act, do everything
in the name of the Lord Jesus, giving *thanks* to God the
Father through him" (Col 3, 15-17). "Persevere in prayer with mind awake and *thankful* heart; and include a
prayer for us, that God may give us an opening for
preaching, to tell the secret of Christ; this indeed is why
I am now in prison. Pray that I may make the secret
plain, as it is my duty to do" (Col 4, 2-4).

We can find here the meaning of the prayer of gratitude. It is first of all Trinitarian. We give thanks to God
the Father through Christ for the gifts he has given,
particularly the gift of faith and the gift of love. We
thank him because he has taken us from the domain of

darkness and brought us into the kingdom of light. He has taken us from the state where sin was our world and brought us into the kingdom of his Son, whose peace we now share, and whose word now dwells within us. As all of our activities now belong to a new world, the world of Christ, they should all be marked with a response fitting this gifted-life. This response is unceasing gratitude.

There are other things we learn about Christian prayer from these verses besides the importance of gratitude. Paul prays for the same gifts here as in the other letters: the gifts of wisdom, understanding, full insight into God's will. In this regard we can recall the remarks we made concerning the discernment of God's will, and the important place it has in Paul's vision of the meaning of the Christian life. He prays that they may always do what is pleasing to God, that they may have the gifts of fortitude, patience, joy, peace. He tells them that they must persevere in prayer. He reminds them that the success of his own apostolate depends on their prayer for him.

He concludes with a greeting from the one who had introduced them to Christ by preaching the Gospel and who continues to pray for them that they stand fast and be wholly devoted to doing God's will. "Greetings from Epaphras, servant of Christ, who is one of yourselves. He prays hard for you all the time, that you may stand fast, ripe in conviction and wholly devoted to doing God's will" (Col 4, 12).

In this letter then we see that the prayer which should characterize the Christian is the prayer of gratitude. This should be the rule of his life. His transformed life comes from the fact that he has been taken from the kingdom of darkness and transferred into the kingdom of the Son, who is the image of the invisible God, the one who has the primacy over all things, the first to return from the dead, the one in whom the fulness of God is embodied. Being united to him should fill the Christian with an unceasing hymn of thanksgiving.

h. The Letter To Philemon (61-63 A.D.)

This short letter is addressed to a fellow Christian whose slave, Philemon, had run away. Paul is sending the slave back to his master, no longer as a slave but as a brother because in the meantime he had become a Christian. "For perhaps this is why you lost him for a time, that you might have him back for good, no longer as a slave, but as more than a slave—as a dear brother, very dear indeed to me and how much dearer to you, both as man and as Christian" (Phm 15-16).

Even in this short letter we find the same spirit of prayer which characterizes Paul's longer letters. There is the prayer of thanks, and the prayer of petition, in which Paul prays (as usual) for deeper union with one another and with Christ. He concludes with a prayer that Christ's peace (a gift which comprises all other gifts) be with Philemon. He also states that his success depends on Philemon's prayers for him.

"Grace to you and peace from God our Father and the Lord Jesus Christ. I *thank* my God always when I mention you in my prayers, for I hear of your love and faith towards the Lord Jesus and towards all God's people. My *prayer* is that your fellowship with us in our common faith may deepen the understanding of all the blessings that our *union with Christ* brings us. For I am delighted and encouraged by your love: through you, my brother, God's people have been refreshed" (Phm 3-7). He concludes, "There is another thing: will you get a place ready for me to stay in? I am hoping *through your prayers* to be restored to you . . . May the grace of our Lord Jesus Christ be with your Spirit" (Ph 22-25).

This short letter is like a gem. It reflects, tiny as it is, a thousand rays of light. It brings out the meaning of our Christian life, which makes us brothers with one another and with Christ. At the same time we see that prayer is as natural to this life as breathing. Even in this short letter which ostensibly has nothing directly to do with prayer we find Paul's own spirit of prayer and his awareness of his dependence on the prayers of a fellow Christian.

i. The Pastoral Letters: 1 Timothy, Titus, 2 Timothy (65 A.D.)

These three letters are addressed to two of Paul's loyal followers. They contain for the most part detailed instructions about the organization, governing, and discipline of the communities entrusted to them. There are also many instructions concerning the nature of their ministry and how they should conduct themselves in the ministry. The advice given to Timothy and Titus is as timely today as it was then.

We find in these letters the same features of prayer as in the other letters. There is only one distinguishing characteristic. Paul here exercises his role as liturgist, that is, as one who directs the worship of the community. In an instruction on community prayer he spells out for them the role which the Christian community has as the intercessor for all men.

We shall treat all three of these letters together. For sake of convenience, we shall first of all consider the passages which bear witness to Paul's own life of prayer, then those in which he teaches something about prayer.

He begins with his usual prayerful greeting. "Grace, mercy, and peace to you from God the Father and Christ Jesus our Lord" (1 Tm 2). This same greeting is repeated in the second letter. In the letter to Titus it is modified slightly. "To Titus, my trueborn son in the faith which we share, grace and peace from God our Father and Christ Jesus our Savior" (Tt 1, 4). His conclusion also is practically the same in all three letters: "Grace be with you all!" (1 Tm and Tt); "Grace be with you all!" (2 Tm).

We find the customary prayer of thanks which is of such paramount importance for him. "I thank him who has made me equal to the task, Christ Jesus our Lord; I thank him for judging me worthy of this trust and appointing me to his service—although in the past I had met him with abuse and persecution and outrage" (1 Tm 1, 12). "I thank God—whom I, like my forefathers, worship with a pure intention—when I mention you in my prayers; this I do constantly night and day" (2 Tm 1, 3). Paul's thanks, therefore, are both for the gifts which God has given to him, and also for what God has given to Timothy. Paul's own debt of gratitude is all the greater because he has been called to be an apostle of the same Christ whom he had previously persecuted.

We find examples of Paul's prayer for others. He prays for his benefactor, Onesiphorus, who had befriended him when everyone else had deserted him. "I pray that the Lord may grant him to find mercy from the Lord on the great Day" (2 Tm 1, 18). Following the exhortation and the example of the Lord to pray for one's enemies, he prayed for a certain Alexander who had done him much harm and for the others who had left him without any assistance in his hour of need: "I pray that it may not be held against them" (2 Tm 4, 16).

We find in these letters three doxologies. They resemble the doxologies which we found in Romans.

The first doxology occurs when Paul remembers the supreme act of mercy shown to him when he himself was forgiven. "Here are words you may trust, words that merit full acceptance: Christ Jesus came into the world to save sinners, and among them I stand first. But I was mercifully dealt with for this very purpose, that Jesus Christ might find in me the first occasion for displaying his patience, and that I might be typical of all who were in future to have faith in him and gain eternal life. Now to the King of the worlds, immortal, invisible, the only God, be honor and glory for ever and ever! Amen" (1 Tm 1, 15-17). The reflection on the workings of God's love and mercy calls forth a comprehensive exclamation of praise. This one sentence sums up the whole of the Jewish faith, but now it is taken into a Christian context. The hymn of praise to God is evoked because of God's mercy to him in his Son. The saving acts of God reach their climax and their complete resolution in the saving acts of Christ.

The second doxology occurs when Paul speaks of the second coming of Christ. He is reminding Timothy to be faithful to his charge to the very end. "Now in the presence of God, who gives life to all things, and of

Jesus Christ, who himself made the same noble confession and gave his testimony to it before Pontius Pilate, I charge you to obey your orders irreproachably and without fault until our Lord Jesus Christ appears. That appearance God will bring to pass in his own good time —God who in eternal felicity alone holds sway. He is King of Kings and Lord of lords; he alone possesses immortality, dwelling in unapproachable light. No man has ever seen or ever can see him. To him be honor and might for ever! Amen" (1 Tm 6, 13—16).

Paul first of all recalls the example of Christ who bore witness to his mission before Pontius Pilate. He should be the model of every Christian, even in bearing witness by one's death to the truth of the faith. In the presence of that same Christ and his Father, Paul exhorts Timothy to discharge his office faithfully and without any fault until the manifestation of Christ. The thought of Christ's final manifestation touches a deep chord in Paul's heart and calls forth the prayer of praise to the majesty of God. In these doxologies we find it is the transcendence of God which is described—his kingship, the fact that he is Lord, immortal, invisible, unapproachable because of the excess of light which envelopes him, out of the reach of the vision of any man. If one considers only the words, these doxologies could have been prayed by a Jew in his worship. What makes them distinctively Christian is their point of departure. This is always the manifestation of God's majesty in and through his Son, Jesus Christ.

The final doxology could refer either to the Father or to Christ. Paul is speaking of the constant assistance with which the Lord protects him. This thought moves him to offer his prayer of praise to the Lord. "But the Lord stood by me and gave me power, so that through me the whole message might be proclaimed for the gentiles to hear; and so I was rescued from the lion's mouth. The Lord will rescue me from all evil attempts on me, and bring me safely to his heavenly kingdom. To him be glory forever and ever. Amen" (2 Tm 4, 17-18). The Lord is always with him, truly the Emmanuel, giving him strength to preach, rescuing him from danger, and finally bringing him to the heavenly kingdom. He is deserving of praise forever and ever because of the way he manifests his saving presence.

As noted above, Paul assumes here his role as one who directs the worship of the community. In the following passage the thought is as usual compact and comprehensive. To do justice to it would require a long commentary. This passage has in fact served as the privileged locus for the reflections of the Fathers and the medieval theologians on the meaning of Christian prayer. The exhortation to pray is given its sound theological basis in God's universal saving will and in the uniqueness of the mediatorship of Christ. Let us quote the entire passage and then make a few observations on it.

"My advice is that, first of all, there should be prayers offered for everyone—petitions, intercessions and thanksgiving—and especially for kings and others in authority, so that we may be able to live religious and reverent lives in peace and quiet. To do this is right, and will please God our savior: he wants all men to be saved and to reach full knowledge of the truth. For there is only one God, and there is only one mediator between God and mankind, himself a man, Christ Jesus, who sacrificed himself as a ransom for them all. He is the evidence of this, sent at the appointed time, and I have been named a herald and apostle of it and—I am telling the truth and no lie—a teacher of the faith and the truth to the pagans. In every place, then, I want the men to lift their hands up reverently in prayer, with no anger or resentment" (1 Tm 2, 1-8).

It will not be out of place here to give an example of the way in which a medieval commentator approaches a Scriptural text. It will help us both to understand the text itself, but even more it shows us the mentality of such commentators. They try to explain Scripture by Scripture. Moreover they try to render a systematic presentation of what is found in an unsystematic way in Scripture. Though their methods are not the same as the modern Scripture scholar, they do have a contribution to make if one is sympathetic to their approach. We shall take as our example a text from St. Thomas. Though he treated this passage at length in his commentary on the First Letter to Timothy, we shall take as our illustrative passage his treatment in his systematic work, the *Summa Theologiae* (II-II, 83, 17).

He asks whether the parts of prayer are aptly divided into entreaties, prayers, petitions, and acts of thanksgiving. The fact that Paul used four different words (*obsecrationes, orationes, postulationes, gratiarum actiones*) provides the point of the departure for the question asked by St. Thomas.

In answer to the question he says that three things are necessary for prayer. The first requirement is that the one who is praying approach God to whom he is directing his prayer. This is what is meant by the word "prayer" (*oratio*) for prayer is the "ascent of the mind to God," which is the definition given by St. John Damascene. Secondly one has to make his petition. This is expressed by the word "petition" (*postulatio*). The petition can be for something explicit, which some call petition in the proper sense of the term, or it can be general, as when one simply asks to be helped by God, which they call supplication (*supplicatio*), or when only the fact is mentioned, as we find in John 11, 3, "Behold, he whom you love is ill." This they call inference (*insinuatio*). The third requirement is that there be a reason for asking. The reason for asking is found both in God and in man. In God it is his holiness, because of which we beg to be heard, as Scripture says, "And now, our God, listen to the prayer and pleading of your servant. For your own sake, Lord, let your face smile again on your desolate sanctuary" (Dn 9, 17-18). Entreaty (*obsecratio*) pertains to this, for entreaty is an earnest prayer through what is holy, as when for example we say, "Through your nativity, deliver us, O Lord." The reason for asking on the part of man is thanksgiving (*gratiarum actiones*), because "being thankful for the gifts we have received, we merit to receive even more precious gifts," as it is said in the collect of the Mass.

St. Thomas then quotes the gloss on the Scripture text. These comments which were made by way of a gloss on the text had great authority among the medieval theologians. Here the gloss on 1 Tim 2, 1, says that "in the Mass entreaties (*obsecrationes*) are those which precede the consecration," in which entreaties certain holy things are recalled to mind; "the prayers (*orationes*) are in the very consecration itself," in which the mind should be supremely elevated to God; "the petitions (*postulationes*), however, are in the petitions which follow; and the thanksgiving (*gratiarum actiones*) comes at the end."

He notes that these four elements can be found in most of the collects of the Mass. In the collect for the Mass of the Trinity, for example, when we say, "Almighty, eternal God," this pertains to the ascent of the mind to God; when we say, "who granted your servants . . . ", this pertains to the act of thanksgiving; the words, "Grant, we beg you," pertain to petition; and what is put at the end, "Through our Lord Jesus Christ . . . ", pertains to entreaty.

We can appreciate to some extent from this example the mentality of the medieval commentator. He would see in Scripture an unformed synthesis of all truths concerning God and man. He would often attempt to make these into a formed synthesis, as in the passage we have referred to. From one verse of Scripture a fairly sophisticated theology of prayer is developed.

Let us return to our text. Perhaps we can understand it best by seeing it from the viewpoint of the convergence of four wills, the will of the Father, the will of Christ, the will of Paul, and the will of the Christian community. All of these wills have only one object, the salvation of all men.

First of all, and most basic, the *will of God* is that all men be saved. He is the only God. He is the only savior, in as much as he is the source and term of all saving acts. Secondly there is the *will of Christ* in his human nature. He is the only mediator. He has effected the salvation of all men through his sacrificial death. He is the evidence of the seriousness of his Father's will to save all men. It is also *Christ's will* that Paul become a herald and apostle of this message. There is, in the third place, *Paul's own will*. He wants these prayers to be offered. He stresses the importance of it by prefacing his remarks with the words "first of all." This is a duty then before all other duties since it is giving evidence to God's own primary desire, the salvation of all men. Then there is the *will of the community* which shows itself in these prayers, the lifting up of their hands and their hearts to God. The will of the Father for the salvation of all men is ultimately the orchestration of these four wills—the Father's, that of Christ, Paul's and the Christian community.

Two other points should be noted about this passage. In the first place it emphasizes the universality of God's saving will; secondly the notion of salvation is related concretely to the Christian faith. Paul first of all asks for prayers for "all men." He singles out those in particular for whom we should pray, sovereigns and those in high office. There is the conviction that prayer can win God's grace and that God's grace can change the hearts of all men. This has always been a constant in both the Jewish and Christian faith. Paul affirms that God's saving will is directed to all men, and that Jesus Christ sacrificed himself to win freedom for all mankind. The genuinity of this will is shown in the fact that Paul was chosen to bear witness to this universal will since he was appointed to bring the gospel to the nations or the Gentiles. A concatenation of wills is thus involved in Paul's understanding of prayer: God's saving will for all men, Christ's redemptive act for all men, the sending of the apostle Paul to all men, and the prayer of the community for all men.

185

The second point which we noted was that Paul's notion of salvation is related concretely to the *Christian* faith. He is not concerned here with the theological problem of how all men can be saved, or how men who do not know the revealed truth in the church can be saved. He is talking about the salvation which is identified with the knowledge of Christ. There is an intimate, essential, casual relationship between salvation and the full knowledge of truth. The knowledge and the truth which Paul is speaking of are not abstractions. He means the acknowledgment of God's saving act in Christ and in the Christian community. In other words he is praying that men become Christians. The question of what happens to those who do not become Christians is not considered by Paul; it was to be taken up by the theologians later. This view, that Paul is praying for the salvation which comes in and through the Christian community, is based on Paul's words, "knowledge of the truth." The word "knowledge" (*epignosis*) is one of Paul's favorites. It is what could be called "affective knowledge," implying a disposition of the heart and not simply the capacity of the mind to know. The word "truth" is another of Paul's favorite words. It is used primarily in the religious sense. The truth of God is shown in his fidelity, especially in sending his Son. The full knowledge of the truth is another way of expressing the full knowledge of God's fidelity in sending his Son. Concretely the act by which this is acknowledged is Christian faith, and the community formed through this acknowledgement is the Christian community.

There are several other points concerning prayer in the pastoral letters. First of all they teach that everything can be sanctified by prayer. Prayer serves as an act of consecration. When it is said over anything or over any action, that action or thing is set aside, is hallowed. He says, "For everything that God created is good, and nothing is to be rejected when it is taken with thanksgiving, since it is hallowed by God's own word and by prayer" (1 Tm 4, 4). He is directing his remarks against those who have a twisted view of the gifts God has given us, particularly in regard to marriage and notions concerning certain foods. He says, "They forbid marriage and inculcate abstinence from certain foods, though God created them to be enjoyed with thanksgiving by believers who have inward knowledge of the truth" (1 Tm 4, 3). The blessing we say over food or over any action sanctifies the food and the action.

We also learn that there were regular times when the community met for prayer and worship. He mentions this when he is describing the kind of life which should characterize those who are widows. "A widow, however, in the full sense, one who is alone in the world, has all her hope set on God, and regularly attends the meetings for prayer and worship night and day" (1 Tm 5, 5).

By way of summary we see in the practical directions given to Timothy and Titus the importance of prayer in the life of the Christian. Paul's own life exemplifies this. The early Christian community had its regular times for prayer and worship. There was no action which could not be sanctified by calling down God's blessing on it. In a special way the Christian community is drawn into Christ's own mediatorship. It becomes the extension of

Christ's own saving act and the way God's will to save all men is brought into focus in space and time. The Christian community is by its very nature an intercessory community, a priestly community.

j. The Letter To The Hebrews (67A.D.)

What we find concerning Christian prayer in Hebrews fits in with what we have already seen in the letters of Paul. Though it is not possible to say with certitude that Paul is the author of this letter. It is generally conceded that the letter is imbued with his spirit. If if did not come directly from him, it came from a kindred mind and heart, perhaps from someone who was informed by Paul's own mentality.

The ideas concerning prayer can be found in the other letters. But one aspect of Christian prayer is highlighted in a special way in this letter. It is the aspect of confidence, a confidence which is at the same time a boldness in approaching the throne of God because the way to him has been opened to us by Christ.

We have already commented on the significance of the word which is translated as "confidence," "boldness" (parrhesia) in the Pauline writings. This same word occurs in Hebrews. It describes the relationship which the Christian has with God because of his relationship to Christ. In particular it describes the attitude that belongs to Christian prayer.

What is the basis for this confidence? It comes from our relationship to Christ, his relationship to us, and his relationship to the Father.

Christ is related to the Father as Son. The first part of

the letter describes this sonship of Christ. "At various times in the past and in various different ways, God spoke to our ancestors through the prophets; but in our own time, the last days, he has spoken to us through his Son, the Son that he has appointed to inherit everything and through whom he made everything there is" (Heb 1, 1-2).

Christ is related to the Christian as brother is related to brother, as a priest is related to those whom he consecrates, and as a member of the same family. "For a consecrating priest and those whom he consecrates are all of one stock; and that is why the Son does not shrink from calling men his brothers....The children of a family share the same flesh and blood; and so he too shared ours, so that through death he might break the power of him who had death at his command, that is, the devil" (Heb 2, 11-12, 14-15). "For every house has its founder; and the founder of all is God. Moses, then, was faithful as a servitor in God's whole household; his task was to bear witness to the words that God would speak; but Christ is faithful as a son, set over his household. And we are that household of his, if only we are *fearless* and keep our hope high" (Heb 3, 4-6).

Our confidence is based mainly on the fact that Christ is our high priest. "For ours is not a high priest unable to sympathize with our weaknesses, but one who, because of his likeness to us, has been tested in every way, only without sin. Let us therefore *boldly* approach the throne of our gracious God, where we may receive mercy and in his grace find timely help" (Heb 4, 15-16). It is based on the nature of that priesthood. "The priesthood which Jesus holds is perpetual, because he remains forever. That is why he is also able to save absolutely those who approach God through him; he is always living to plead on their behalf" (Heb 7, 24-25). It is based on the fact that Jesus is not only priest; he is also victim. By his blood we are cleansed. "So now, my friends, the blood of Jesus makes us free to enter *boldly* into the sanctuary by the new, living way which he has opened for us through the curtain, the way of the flesh. We have, moreover, a great priest set over the household of God; so let us make our approach in sincerity of heart and full assurance in faith, our guilty hearts sprinkled clean, our bodies washed with pure water. Let us be firm and unswerving in the confession of our hope, for the Giver of the promise may be trusted" (Heb 10, 19-23). He encourages them not to give up their confidence. "Do not throw away your *confidence*, for it carries a great reward" (Heb 10, 35).

This confidence is not based on something which can be changed or in any way shaken by the mutability of time. It is not based on what is passing. The Old Covenant belongs to the things that are passing; the New Covenant endures forever. "No, you stand before Mount Zion and the city of the living God, heavenly Jerusalem, before myriads of angels, the full concourse and assembly of the first-born citizens of heaven, and God the judge of all, and the spirits of good men made perfect, and Jesus the mediator of a new covenant .... The kingdom we are given is unshakable (Heb 12, 22-24, 28).

We are taught the necessity for reverence in our prayer. "Let us hold on to the grace that has been given us, and so worship him as he would be worshipped, with reverence and awe; for our God is a devouring fire" (Heb 12, 29). In our comments on prayer in the New

Testament we have not given explicit attention to the necessity of reverence. The fact that it is not mentioned very often in the New Testament is silent testimony that it was simply taken for granted. If prayer is listening and response, then reverence is the translation of this prayerful attitude into our whole demeanor. It does not mean stiffness, artificiality, or sanctimoniousness. These belong to sophisticated persons. To be reverent one must become a little child.

We have seen the need of confidence in the synoptics' teaching on Christian prayer. It is chiefly in the Hebrews that we learn the *basis* for this confidence. It is rooted in Christ's identification with us through his consecrating act as priest. We belong to him. We have been sprinkled with his blood, and this has set up a bond of kinship. We can enter with boldness and confidence into the presence of the Father because of this kinship with Christ. We need not fear that this relationship will be shaken. It is founded on the perpetual priesthood of Christ.

Christian prayer is offered to the Father through Christ. "Through Jesus, then, let us continually offer up to God the sacrifice of praise, that is, the tribute of lips which acknowledge his name, and never forget to show kindness and to share what you have with others; for such are the sacrifices which God approves" (Heb 13, 15-16). He is careful to point out that our prayer shows itself not only in the sacrifice of praise of our lips, but also through the sacrifice of our charity towards others, even sharing what we have with others. Not only is our prayer of petition offered to the Father through Christ, but also our prayer of praise. The psalms on the lips of the Christian always terminate at least implicitly with the words "through Christ our Lord."

The author shows the value he places on intercessory prayer when he asks them to pray for him. "Pray for us? for we are convinced that our conscience is clear; our one desire is always to do what is right. All the more earnestly I ask for your prayers, that I may be restored to you the sooner" (Heb 13, 19).

Finally, he prays for them. His own prayer ends with a doxology in praise of Christ. "I pray that the God of peace, who brought our Lord Jesus back from the dead to become the great Shepherd of the sheep by the blood that sealed an eternal covenant, may make you ready to do his will in any kind of good action; and may he make of us what he would have us to be through Jesus Christ, to whom be glory forever and ever. Amen....Grace be with you all" (Hebrew 13, 20-21, 25).

The conclusion of the letter is at one and the same time a beautiful prayer and a compendium of the Christian faith. The work of salvation is initiated by the God of peace. This plan of salvation is carried out through the blood of Christ. But God's design does not end with the death of Christ; he brings him back to life. Now he enters into his role as the great Shepherd, leading his flock within the bonds of a new an eternal covenant, to his Father, the God of peace. If we are to belong to the Shepherd, we have to allow ourselves to be led by him; we have to be found like him, by doing his will. In this way we become the design which the Father wants us to be. The doxology is given to Christ to whom belongs the glory forever and ever for having initiated the eternal covenant.

By way of summary we see that Hebrews gives the ultimate reason for the Christian's confidence, his boldness, in approaching the Father: Christ has identified himself with us, redeemed us with his blood, and become our high priest whose priesthood endures forever. No greater reason for confidence could be found. It is based on the definitive revelation of God's love. Nothing can supersede this revelation. Our confidence is based on a love which can never be revoked, a love perpetuated in the high priestly office of Christ which endures forever.

6. The Letters To All Christians

Seven letters in the New Testament are called the "Catholic Epistles." They were not addressed to any particular community but to the community at large or to the whole Church. Three of these are attributed to John, two to Peter and the other two to James and Jude.

The first characteristic of prayer in these letters is a consciousness of God as our Father. The Christian should be aware that God is the source of every gift. "If any of you falls short in wisdom, he should ask God for it and it will be given him, for God is a generous giver who neither refuses nor reproaches anyone. But he must ask in faith, without a doubt in his mind; for the doubter is like a heaving sea ruffled by the wind. A man of that kind must not expect the Lord to give him anything; he is double-minded, and never can keep a steady course" (Jm 1, 5-8). "All good giving and every perfect gift comes from above, from the Father of all light; with him there is no such thing as alteration, no shadow of a change" (Jm 1, 16-17).

To have faith here is synonymous with being single-minded. It is not to some emotional stability or instability which James is referring. He is speaking of the single-mindedness which belongs to the awareness we have through faith that God is our Father, the source of every gift.

Putting this in another way he says that we do not get what we ask for because we do not have the right motives when we pray. "You do not get what you want, because you do not pray for it. Or, if you do, your requests are not granted because you pray from the wrong motives, to spend what you get on your pleasures" (Jm 4, 2-3). Some things come to us, then, only because we pray for them. Some things we pray for we do not receive because we want them only to indulge our own desires, not to bring us closer to God and to others.

Prayer should characterize our whole life, whether we are sad or happy, whether we are ill or well. Our prayer will be more efficacious if we ourselves are holy. "Is anyone among you in trouble? He should turn to prayer. Is anyone in good heart? He should sing praises. Is one of you ill? He should send for the elders of the congregation to pray over him and anoint him with oil in the name of the Lord. The prayer offered in faith will save the sick man, the Lord will raise him from his bed, and any sins he may have committed will be forgiven. Therefore confess your sins to one another, and pray for one another, and then you will be healed. A good man's prayer is powerful and effective. Elijah was a man with human frailties like our own; and when he prayed earnestly that there should be no rain, not a drop fell on the land for three years and a half; then he prayed again, and down came the rain and the land bore crops once more" (Jm 5, 13-18).

We should approach God with confidence. "We can approach God with confidence (*parrhesia*) for this reason: if we make requests which accord with his will he listens to us; and, knowing that whatever we may ask, he hears us, we know that we have already been granted what we asked of him" (1 Jn 5, 14-15). We have already seen the importance of this notion in the letters of Paul, especially in Hebrews. We have the confidence that God hears us if we ask for what is according to his will.

Even if we have failed to do his will, we should not lose confidence. We have someone to plead our cause with the Father: "But should anyone commit a sin, we have one to plead our cause with the Father, Jesus Christ, and he is just. He is himself the remedy for the defilement of our sins, not our sins only but the sins of all the world" (1 Jn 1, 1-2). This motive for confidence is very much like the motives given in Hebrews. It is based on the continuation of Christ's priestly office for us in heaven.

Christian prayer is an exercise of the priestly office that belongs to each Christian in virtue of his baptism. "Come, and let yourselves be built, as living stones, into a spiritual temple; become a holy priesthood, to offer spiritual sacrifices acceptable to God through Jesus Christ . . . . But you are a chosen race, a royal priesthood, a dedicated nation, and a people claimed by God for his own, to proclaim the triumphs of him who has called you out of darkness into his marvelous light. You are now the people of God, who once were not his people; outside his mercy once, you have now received his mercy" (1 P 2, 5, 9-10). Just as the temple of the Israelites was the place of worship and prayer, so the Christian as an individual and as a new people or new community of God becomes the special place, the spiritual temple, where prayer is offered. Similarly just as the priests of the Old Covenant offered the prayers of the people to God, so must the Christian who belongs to the royal priesthood of the New Covenant offer his prayer to God. As temple and as priest the Christian has a special vocation to pray.

Our prayer should include our enemies also. We should repay injury with a blessing, a prayer for the one who injures us. "do not repay wrong with wrong, or abuse with abuse; on the contrary, retaliate with a blessing, for a blessing is the inheritance to which you yourselves have been called (1 P 3, 9).

We should pray also for the sinner. "If anybody sees his brother commit a sin that is not a deadly sin, he has only to pray, and God will give life to the sinner—not those who commit a deadly sin; for there is a sin that is death, and I will not say that you must pray about that. Every kind of wrong-doing is sin, but not all sin is deadly" (1 Jn 5, 16, 17). The sin unto death is probably the sin against truth, a disposition so hardened that it approaches the condition of will that belongs to the evil spirits. In practice, however, this advice is largely hypothetical, because no human person can judge the degree to which another person's will is fixed in evil. The supposition we should act on is that there is a radical openness in the will of everyone which can be gradually brought to fruition through the help of the prayer of another.

Prayer is not some kind of magical influence on God.

There is a correlation between the holiness of our lives and the efficacy of our prayer. "A good man's prayer is powerful and effective" (Jm 5, 16).

The fact that the Christian is living in the last age should make him more intent on prayer. "The end of all things is upon us, so you must lead an ordered and sober life, given to prayer" (1 P 4, 7). The right ordering of married life will also lead to prayer. "In the same way, you husbands must conduct your married life with understanding: pay honor to the woman's body, not only because it is weaker, but also because you share together in the grace of God which gives you life. Then your prayers will not be hindered" (1 P 3, 7) We saw above (cf. 1 Co 7, 5) how Paul spoke of the use or non-use of their marriage rights in the context of greater freedom to pray.

Finally we are reminded of a basic characteristic of Christian prayer which we have found throughout the New Testament. We are empowered to pray through the gift of the Holy Spirit. "Continue to pray in the power of the Holy Spirit" (Jude 20).

These letters also contain the prayerful expression of the author's desires for the Christian community. These prayers form the introduction and conclusion of the letters, and also find expression in the prayers of praise, the doxologies. "Grace and peace to you in fullest measure. Praise be to the God and Father of our Lord Jesus Christ, who in his mercy gave us new birth into a living hope by the resurrection of Jesus Christ from the dead" (1 P 1, 2-3). In all things so act that the glory may be God's through Jesus Christ; to him belong glory and power forever and ever. Amen" (1 P 4, 11). "Peace to you all who belong to Christ" (1 P 5, 14). "Grace and peace be yours in fullest measure, through the knowledge of God and Jesus our Lord" (2 P 1, 2). "But grow in the grace and in the knowledge of our Lord and Savior Jesus Christ. To him be glory now and for all eternity!" (2 P 3, 18). "I pray that you may enjoy good health and that all may go well with you, as I know it goes well with your soul" (3 Jn 2). "Mercy, peace, and love be yours in fullest measure" (Jude 2). "Now to the One who can keep you from falling and set you in the presence of his glory, jubilant and above reproach, to the only God our Savior, be glory and majesty, might and authority, through Jesus Christ our Lord, before all time, now, and for evermore. Amen" (Jude 24-25).

In these prayers we find the same earnest desires that characterize the other writings of the New Testament. These desires are expressed in prayer—prayer for peace, that peace which comes from the knowledge of God and Jesus Christ; prayer that they might grow in this knowledge; prayer for the fulfilment of every need of soul and body; the prayer of praise both to Christ and to the Father through Christ.

Conclusion

From what we have seen in the New Testament concerning prayer, it is easy to apply the words concerning the whole of the new creation specifically to prayer itself. "Then the One sitting on the throne spoke: 'Now I am making the whole of creation new' he said" (Rv 21, 5). The prayer proper to man as man, the prayer proper to the people of God of the Old Testament—these are made completely new. There is some similarity in these three modes of prayer—the prayer of an uncovenanted people, that which comes from the Old Covenant, and that from the New. But the prayer of the New Testament is informed by a new life; it is part of the New Creation. It is the voice of the new creature, in his new relationship to the Father as a son with the Son, through a new gift of the Spirit. His prayer is concerned with the new creation—praise to God for what he has accomplished in Christ, thanksgiving for having brought us into this new creation, petition for the gifts of grace and nature which will bring this creation to fruition, blessings which draw every action and everything in the old creation into the new.

It is literally true to say that the whole of the New

Testament is saturated with the spirit of prayer. No matter who the author, no matter what the subject matter, no matter what the audience, in every book and letter of the New Testament there are examples of Christians at prayer, explicit teaching on prayer, and exhortation to pray. This can only be explained by the gift of the Spirit which belongs to the new era. The new creature no sooner comes into existence than he begins to speak with a new tongue, with a new insistence, and with a new confidence.

What is true of those who have been given the Spirit is particularly true of the one who was filled with the Spirit, Christ himself. We have seen that Luke describes the life of Jesus as surrounded and enveloped by the aura of prayer. What happened when Jesus stayed behind in Jerusalem and was found in the temple was only a symbolic externalization of an invisible relationship—the relationship of Christ to his Father. He was always about his Father's business or in the place of his Father, the temple. The temple was the special place of man's encounter with the living God. But the place of meeting which supersedes the temple is Jesus himself. Mark presents Jesus as praying on particular occasions, expecially before major decisions that have to do with the founding of his kingdom. But Luke portrays Jesus as moving in the atmosphere of prayer. It seems to be like seeing the light of the moon. While it shines on our world and is a part of it, we are aware that there is another aspect of the moon, an aspect we never see, one that is surrounded by darkness, an aspect that relates it to the infinite universe beyond. So it is with the prayer of Christ. His face is always towards men, and at the same time we are conscious that he can be turned towards us only because he is enveloped in the darkness and hiddenness of his relationship to the Father. Luke makes us conscious of this side of Christ's life which lies over the horizon of our vision and our experience.

We would only have soundings of the nature of this communion with the Father unless Jesus himself were pleased to describe it in human speech. He has given us this in the prayer he offered to the Father when he exulted in the Holy Spirit (Lk 10, 21), and in his High Priestly Prayer at the Last Supper (Jn 17).

The prayer of the Christian has its value because it is drawn into Christ's double relationship—with his face turned to the Father in the communion he has with him as Son, and his face turned toward men in the communion he has with them as brother and as first-born from the dead. Anything said about the prayer of the Christian in the New Testament derives its force from this relationship. The need for prayer, the characteristics of prayer, the kinds of prayer—all of these derive from the fact that the Christian is in a minor key what Christ is in the major key.

He "has to" pray because Christ "had to" pray. He had to pray to the Father because this is the expression of his relationship to his Father, the expression of his very identity as Son. He had to say what he himself was, a Son. He had to acknowledge through praise the gift and the design of the Father in bringing about the new creation. He had to pray for men, for he was their Savior, High Priest, and Mediator. For the same reasons the Christian has to pray. He has to say what he is, through prayer. He has to acknowledge the goodness of God through thanks and praise in conceiving and carrying out the design of our salvation. He has to pray for others, even for enemies, as Christ himself prayed.

The characteristics of the Christian's prayer will be those of 'Christ's prayer. It will proceed from a pure motive, that the loving will of the Father be done and that his kingdom might come on earth as it is in heaven. It will be constant, as his love is constant. It will be humble, because we are servants with the Servant. It will sometimes be suffering prayer, prayer in agony, with the prayer of the Suffering Servant.

The prayer of the Christian will assume the same forms Christ's prayer had—petition, thanks, praise, intercession. Just as prayer is the register of all the desires Christ had, so Christian prayer will be the register of all he wants for others, himself, and the kingdom of Christ. There is only one form prayer takes in the Christian that it could never take in Christ. That is the prayer for forgiveness of one's own sins. Christ prayed for the forgiveness of others as their High Priest, but he himself was sinless. He is the Redeemer, not one of the redeemed.

The prayer of Christ proceeded from union with the Father: a union of knowledge, a union of love, a union which we lack words to describe because it is so intimate and so complete. It proceeded, then, from a *seeing*, not from a non-seeing. Christ's prayer did not proceed from faith, the kind of union which belongs to the Christian. Faith is both a seeing, and a non-seeing. It is seeing through a mirror darkly. This differentiates Christian prayer, then, from the prayer of Christ.

When the prayer of Christ, the prayer of the Son, becomes the prayer of the adopted son, the Christian, it thus takes on all of the characteristics of the prayer of Christ, insofar as these can be assumed by one who is a sinner, living in time, but living in union with the Risen Lord.

The prayer of the Christian also differs from the prayer of Christ because it is both offered to Christ, and to the Father through Christ. It is obvious that Christ could not pray to himself or through himself. But Christian prayer is always meditated prayer, that is, it bears the marks of Christ's mediation. Whether one says so explicitly or not, it is always offered through Christ. It can also be offered to Christ, whether it is the prayer of thanks and petition, or that of praise and adoration (which we find chiefly in *Revelation*).

These remarks should serve to summarize our study of the New Testament understanding of prayer. If we could sum up all we have said in one sentence, we might say that Christian prayer is Christ's prayer, in and through his members, because these members are united with him through the same Spirit. Ultimately it is the Spirit of Christ who is orchestrating this vast harmony of prayer in the hearts and on the tongues of the Church throughout the world and throughout all time. What the poet, Gerard Manley Hopkins, says about the presence of Christ in human persons, is particularly appropriate when it is applied to Christ praying in his members.

"For Christ plays in ten thousand places,
Lovely in limbs, and lovely in eyes not his
To the Father through the features of men's faces."